— Praise for *Cracking the Man Code* —

"Mat Boggs brings a rare and beautiful combination of emotional intelligence, grounded masculine insight, and deep respect for women to his work. In *Cracking the Man Code*, he offers women a powerful, compassionate, and truly effective road map for cultivating healthy love. I've long appreciated Mat's work, and this book is a gift to anyone ready to receive the love they deserve."

—Katherine Woodward Thomas, MA, MFT, *New York Times* bestselling author of *Calling In the One* and *Conscious Uncoupling*

"*Cracking the Man Code* is a heart-expanding, soul-awakening guide for any woman ready to call in—or elevate—a truly extraordinary relationship. With wisdom, humor, and profound clarity, Mat Boggs lovingly demystifies the male heart, helping women not only understand men better but also reconnect with their own feminine radiance. This book is a beautiful bridge between the soulful and the strategic. It's like having a relationship coach, best friend, and divine wingman all rolled into one."

—Arielle Ford, *New York Times* bestselling author of *The Soulmate Secret* and *Turn Your Mate Into Your Soulmate*

"In *My Fair Lady*, professor Henry Higgins sings a song titled, 'Why can't a woman be more like a man?' and this sums up the reason Mat Boggs's book is so valuable. Women, on the other hand, have thought and said for centuries, 'Why can't he be like my female friends?'

Women and men are different! Mat cracks the code of differences and helps us understand the opposite gender. Thank goodness Mat is so enlightened that he can illuminate the path to love for everyone. If you want to attract your soulmate, let Mat guide your steps to long-lasting love rather than trying to change him to be like a woman!"

—Dr. Chérie Carter-Scott, MCC, #1 *New York Times* bestselling author of *If Life Is a Game, These Are the Rules* and *If Love Is a Game, These Are the Rules*

"Sis, let me say this loud and clear—*Cracking the Man Code* is a game changer! The ideas in this book helped me create the love I have today. Mat Boggs doesn't just teach dating advice—he teaches soul alignment, masculine/feminine harmony, and how to show up as the powerful woman you are. This book is your permission slip to stop guessing, start receiving, and attract a man who honors you deeply."

—Lisa Nichols, *New York Times* bestselling author of *No Matter What* and featured teacher in *The Secret*

"What I love most about *Cracking the Man Code* is that it's not just theory—it's actionable, loving, and profoundly effective, offering a road map to create lasting, soul-satisfying love. Mat Boggs demystifies the male mind in a way that's empowering for women. If you've ever wanted to create a stronger connection, experience greater passion, or feel deeply seen by your partner, this book is a perfect guide. Inspiring, enlightening, and a total joy to read."

—Marci Shimoff, #1 *New York Times* bestselling author of *Love for No Reason* and *Happy for No Reason*

"Reading *Cracking the Man Code* is like having your smartest, kindest guy friend finally decode what men are really thinking—without the eye-roll clichés or fake advice. Mat brings the truth with humor, vulnerability, and that irresistible 'good guy' charm that makes you trust every word."

—Marni Battista, author of *Your Radical Living Challenge* and founder of Dating with Dignity

"This book is like a glass of wine, a box of dark chocolate, and your best girlfriend telling you the truth—wrapped into one! *Cracking the Man Code* is smart, sexy, and spot-on. Mat Boggs has a rare gift for helping women understand men without ever asking us to shrink or settle. This is the kind of love guidance we all should've gotten years ago!"

—Dr. Anna Cabeca, The Girlfriend Doctor and national bestselling author of *The Hormone Fix*

— Praise for Mat Boggs —

"I'm living proof this works. I took Mat's Manifest Your Man course, applied the principles in this book, and I manifested my husband. Not just any man—but a man who sees me, cherishes me, and meets me fully. *Cracking the Man Code* is the real deal. It shifted how I showed up, and everything changed. If you're dreaming of true love, start here."

—Sharon Vidano, retired lawyer, life mastery consultant, and Manifest Your Man graduate

"Mat delivers practical advice to help you break down emotional walls, communicate with more compassion, and open the door for deeper intimacy in your relationship—without nagging or nitpicking. If you're looking for better ways to connect with the man you love, you need this on your shelf."

—Alex Cattoni, married woman, entrepreneur, and founder of the Copy Posse

"I manifested the love of my life while taking Mat Boggs's amazing coaching program. The strategies in *Cracking the Man Code* that Mat provided me transformed years of unsuccessful dating into the opportunity to cultivate and develop a relationship which will last for the rest of my life. These strategies helped me create a mindset that overcame all the negative thoughts and influences that were preventing me from creating the relationship I was seeking."

—Linda Keating, retired and traveling with the man of her dreams

"I was a single mom at 40 and my daughter became my first miracle. By the time my daughter was grown, I prayed to God for a second miracle. With Mat's coaching and *Cracking the Man Code*, it gave me the belief, clarity, confidence, and understanding of how to attract the man of my dreams. With Mat's wisdom and advice, I did just that and today I am blessed to be in the most loving relationship of my life—one that feels like coming home. I am forever grateful."

—Aurelie Catherine Cormier, Needham, MA, Manifest Your Man graduate

Cracking the MAN CODE

— Also by Mat Boggs —

Project Everlasting

Cracking the MAN CODE

Unlock the Mystery of HOW MEN THINK, LOVE, AND COMMUNICATE to Create the Relationship You've Always Wanted

MAT BOGGS

BenBella Books, Inc.
Dallas, TX

BenBella Books, Inc.
8080 N. Central Expressway
Suite 1700
Dallas, TX 75206
benbellabooks.com
Send feedback to feedback@benbellabooks.com

BenBella is a federally registered trademark.

Printed in the United States of America
10 9 8 7 6 5 4 3 2 1

Library of Congress Control Number: 2025042186
ISBN 9781637748237 (trade paperback)
ISBN 9781637748244 (electronic)

Editing by Rebecca Pillsbury and Claire Schulz
Copyediting by Elizabeth Degenhard
Proofreading by Sarah Vostok and Marissa Wold Uhrina
Text design and composition by Aaron Edmiston
Cover design by Sarah Avinger
Cover image © Adobe Stock / Esin Deniz
Printed by Lake Book Manufacturing

To Irene, the love of my life

Contents

Foreword by Gay Hendricks, PhD xiii
Introduction xv

PART ONE
Discovering Polarity:
The One Thing That Changes Everything

Chapter One The Twin Energies of Attraction 3
Chapter Two Masculine and Feminine:
A Tale of Two Energies 13
Chapter Three Befriending His Inner Caveman 27

PART TWO
Igniting Attraction

Chapter Four Becoming Irresistible:
There's Just Something About Her 43
Chapter Five His Deepest Desire 59
Chapter Six His Greatest Fear 73
Chapter Seven Stay True to Your Standards 81

PART THREE

Deepening Connection

Chapter Eight	The Alchemy of Sex Drive: Mr. Miami Goes to Seattle	**93**
Chapter Nine	The Ultimate Connection Code: What His Heart Longs For	**109**

PART FOUR

Speaking the Language of His Heart

Chapter Ten	The Art of MANguistics	**127**
Chapter Eleven	Transforming Conflict into Closeness	**145**
	A Final Message	**169**
	Acknowledgments	**175**
	Cracking the Man Code Resources	**179**
	Notes	**183**

Foreword

It is my great pleasure to present to you a book I predict will become a classic in the field of relationship transformation: Mat Boggs's *Cracking the Man Code*. The book brings a wealth of new wisdom to a matter of timeless importance: how to attract the love of your life and create a thriving relationship over time.

As I began reading, I was greeted by a happy surprise. Although *Cracking the Man Code* speaks directly to its primary audience of women, it's filled with wisdom that's also of great value to men. Throughout the book, I experienced many "A-HA!" moments as I discovered new things about myself as a man.

Cracking the Man Code is full of big ideas, some of which may stretch your current thinking about men and women. For example, Mat's explanation of masculine and feminine energies—which transcend gender—and the role of polarity in attraction will revolutionize your approach to relationships. The book also offers a bridge across the gulf that often exists when women and men communicate, especially when they don't realize how their words and actions affect each other. These ideas—just a few of the many Mat shares—will be life-changing for women seeking to attract love and keep it growing through the years. And for every idea, there are one or more true stories to make the theoretical come to life!

In my opinion, it's this rich array of engaging stories that makes this book really shine. Because Mat has been teaching these concepts in workshops for many years, he's accumulated a wealth of up-close examples of how women have used his principles and tools to create lasting love. Some of the stories had me in tears, some made me chuckle, some made me think. Whether they made me laugh or cry, the stories all have one thing in common: they come straight from the heart.

To top it off, *Cracking the Man Code* brings its paradigm-shifting principles into practical action through a set of ingenious tools, which are clear, simple, and easy to apply—whether you're single or already in a committed relationship. You don't have to wait until you've finished the book to put these tools to work and start seeing positive results.

It's for all these reasons I highly recommend *Cracking the Man Code*. The concepts and tools presented in its pages are genuinely empowering to women and succeed admirably in doing what its subtitle promises: to show you "how men think, love, and communicate to create the relationship you've always wanted."

—Gay Hendricks, PhD, author of
The Big Leap* and *Conscious Loving

Introduction

— The Sweat, the Sushi, and the Spark —

The butterflies in my stomach were throwing a full-on rave. I sat in the driver's seat of a rented Toyota Corolla, heart pounding, palms sweating, staring over at the woman sitting in my passenger seat.

Her name was Irene. Gorgeous, graceful, the kind of presence that makes you forget your own name. This was our first date. I'd flown from Oregon to Southern California just to see her. Now, here I was, trying to play it cool, when a moment came that should have been simple, but wasn't.

"So," I said, flashing what I hoped was a confident grin, completely unaware I was walking into a trap of my own making, "where do you want to go to dinner?"

Irene tilted her head, raised an eyebrow, and gave me a smile that was both kind and curious.

"You don't have a place picked out?"

Wait, what? I blinked. "No," I said, chuckling nervously. "I figured since this is your town, you'd know the best spots."

She smiled again, but there was something else in her eyes now. Something I couldn't quite place. Maybe a flicker of surprise. Maybe amusement.

"But you asked *me* out," she said gently. "Don't you usually make a plan when you take someone on a date?"

Oof. Her question landed like a sucker punch to my gut. I could feel the heat rising in my body. My neck flushed. My hands started to get clammy. And right there, under her soft gaze and in the gentle silence that followed her question . . . I froze. Beads of sweat started forming on my forehead. I had no idea where to take her. It hit me like that childhood moment when I was halfway to school and realized I'd left my science project on the kitchen counter.

What happened next changed everything. But before I tell you what unfolded in that moment, I want to take you back. Way back. Because this date wasn't just a date. It was the culmination of a journey I'd been on since I was a kid.

The Heart of a Romantic

At eight years old, I was already a hopeless romantic. While most of the boys in my class were obsessed with riding their BMX bikes, leveling up in *Super Mario Bros.*, or trying to build backyard forts with plywood and a questionable sense of engineering, I was daydreaming about my future wife.

I grew up on a farm in a little town called Scholls, just outside of Portland, Oregon. Picture acres of rolling land, fruit trees, and more than a few splinters. And while the world outside was tractors and tree swings, inside our home was something entirely different.

My mom was a well-known minister and a global leader in the personal development world. She led a large New Thought church in Portland and taught transformational principles to people all over the world. While most kids my age were learning cheat codes for Nintendo, I was learning the power of intention and how to breathe through my feelings. And yes, I still snuck in a little Mario and fort building when I could.

But love? That was my main mission, which my older brothers did *not* let me forget. I had a habit of talking in my sleep—and not just any kind of sleep talk. I'd murmur the name of whatever girl I had a crush on at the time, wearing a lovesick smile like I'd just walked out of a Hallmark movie. I was a tiny Romeo in Transformers pajamas. At breakfast, over bowls of Frosted Mini-Wheats at the kitchen table, my brothers would go into full performance mode—hands over their hearts, dramatic sighs—using whatever name they'd heard me say the night before: "Oh, Julie . . . Oh, Julie . . ." They'd drag the scene out like a bad soap opera, laughing as I turned bright red and told them to knock it off.

And that was just the beginning.

At fifteen, while most teenagers were spending their weekends at the mall or pumping nickels into games at Wonderland arcade, I was sitting in the back of hotel ballrooms at my mom's personal growth seminars. She'd hand me a name tag and a notebook and give me a hug, then I'd reluctantly take my seat.

Since my mom was the one onstage leading the whole thing, I felt I had to play full out. I nodded earnestly, took notes, and did the eye-gazing exercises. One weekend, I found myself sitting knee to knee with a forty-five-year-old man named Bob during an emotional breakthrough exercise.

Bob, voice trembling, eyes tearing, opened up about the pain of his recent divorce. I nodded, doing my best to hold eye contact without totally imploding inside. Then it was my turn. I started sharing my "deep emotional wound"— Sarah, the girl I'd been dating (as much as a ninth grader could "date"), had just dumped me for Manny. He was older. Cooler. The guy who threw parties and probably had a fake ID. I, on the other hand, was the guy who played it safe—straightlaced-ish, generally polite, and rocking a church attendance record my mom was very proud of.

Bob patted my shoulder like we were battle-worn brothers. The whole thing was deeply uncomfortable. I didn't love being vulnerable with strangers. But those moments—and the countless others like them while I was growing up—planted a seed. Years later, after a few more heart-wrenching breakups in my twenties, that early exposure to personal growth came rushing back. And this time, those experiences gave me clarity. If all my relationships were ending the same way, maybe it wasn't just bad luck. Maybe the common denominator was . . . *me*.

That realization didn't crush me—it *compelled* me. I needed answers. By the time I hit my late twenties, I'd racked up enough failed relationships to know something wasn't working. I kept attracting women I wasn't all that interested in, while the ones I *did* like seemed to disappear faster than my Nintendo controller during sibling fights. So I did what any love-ambitious, personal growth–trained, slightly desperate guy would do: I launched a full-scale investigation.

My best friend Jason and I packed up an RV and traveled across the country interviewing couples who had been happily married for forty years or more. We called them the *Marriage Masters*, and we asked them everything: What makes love last? What makes it fade? What would you do differently if you could go back? We listened to stories of devotion, heartbreak, forgiveness, and laughter. These couples had weathered life's biggest storms—and stayed in love. The insights they shared opened my eyes to the unconscious patterns I'd been repeating in my own relationships. That journey became our book, *Project Everlasting: Two Bachelors Discover the Secrets of America's Greatest Marriages.* Suddenly, we were being invited to speak on stages, sharing what we—as self-proclaimed "love-clueless guys"—had learned from the real experts: the couples who'd done the work and made love last.

And that's when something unexpected happened. Backstage at many of these events, I overheard conversations between authors and psychologists. They were tossing around a concept I'd never heard before: *polarity.* The idea that every romantic relationship is made up of two core energies—masculine and feminine—and that those energies either attract or repel depending on how they're expressed. At first, it just sounded like more theory. But then something clicked. It was like someone held up a mirror to my love life and said, "Hey, man, this is what you've been missing." My mind went full *tilt*.

I'd always prided myself on being a good guy—respectful, kind, and collaborative. But what I didn't realize was that the *way* I was expressing those qualities often placed me in the feminine role without even knowing it. I would wait for women to show interest. Wait for women to take the lead. Ask *them* to choose where we went, what we did, even what the relationship meant. And then I wondered why they didn't feel attraction.

So, I dove in. I read books by authors like Alison Armstrong, John Gray, David Deida, and Gay and Kathlyn Hendricks; listened to any audios I could find (there weren't many); and started experimenting with the idea of embodying more of my masculine energy—that grounded, decisive presence that makes a woman feel safe enough to soften into her feminine energy. (And no, I don't mean by being macho or domineering—we'll unpack the real thing soon.)

Cracking the Code

Which brings us back to Irene. After meeting her at an expo in California while doing a book signing, I consciously decided to flip the script. Instead of waiting to be approached, I walked up to her. I leaned in, struck up a conversation, and pursued her. And it worked: She paid attention. We exchanged contact information and, over time, made plans for our first date.

On our first date, I *wanted* to show up differently. But old habits die hard. There I was, in the driver's seat of my rental Toyota, unconsciously slipping back into a familiar old pattern—leaning back, deferring, handing off the direction of the evening. Not because I didn't care or wasn't interested. And definitely not because I didn't value Irene's input—of course I did. But for most of my dating life, I'd been conditioned to stay neutral. To be easygoing. To go with the flow, which more often than not looked like letting my date be the one to guide the experience.

And here she was, offering me something I'd never experienced quite like this before—a beautiful, feminine invitation to do something different. To step forward. To lead.

"Don't you usually make a plan when you take someone on a date?" she'd asked.

I needed a place to take her for dinner, and fast. I was mentally scrambling. I grabbed my phone, opened Yelp, and started frantically searching.

Irene felt the anxious energy I was giving off. She smiled again, softer this time, and said, "I like sushi or Italian. Either one is great." That one sentence was like a lighthouse in the fog. She wasn't trying to take control; she was giving me the space to make a decision.

"Sushi," I said.

She smiled.

I found a 4.5-star place a few miles away, threw the car into drive, and off we went. The restaurant was amazing—great food, cozy atmosphere, the whole vibe just clicked. Partway through dinner, Irene looked up from her plate and said, "Thank you. This place is fantastic."

Then I felt it. That burst of appreciation, of feeling her happiness in response to my leadership. It was electric, like I had unlocked a part of myself that had been dormant for years.

I didn't know it at the time, but that moment would mark the beginning of a new chapter in my life. A chapter where I would go even deeper into studying polarity, masculine and feminine energy, and what it takes to create and sustain passionate, connected love. That first date had its bumpy moments and beautiful breakthroughs. But it also became the first page in the greatest love story of my life—one that has been going strong for more than eighteen years.

Who This Book Is For (and Why It's Different)

After *Project Everlasting* came out (and after I experienced firsthand how the principles of polarity could transform a love life), something surprising started happening. Women—smart, successful, amazing women—started reaching out from all over the world. Some wrote emails. Some found me on social media. Some approached me after speaking events with a spark in their eyes and *real frustration* in their voices.

"Mat, I love what you shared from the Marriage Masters, but where do I meet a man like that? I'm ready for that kind of love, but it feels impossible to find."

Others already in relationships quietly pulled me aside. "Can you help me understand my husband? How do I get him to open up? To step forward? To stop shutting down or pulling away when I try to connect?"

Whether they were single, dating, or married for years, I understood that the questions these women were asking all pointed to the same ache: **How do I create a love that lasts—one that's deeply aligned with who I am and what I truly desire?**

That question lit a fire in me. As cofounder of the Brave Thinking Institute and founder of its Love & Relationships division (a transformational coaching company whose purpose is to empower people to create and live a life they love), this topic has become my life's work. Over the last seventeen-plus years, I've been blessed to serve more than 200 million people through my videos, to speak on stages across the globe, and to personally coach more than one thousand women on their journey to lasting love.

But the more I taught, the more I realized something: There are a lot of great books out there on relationships that are deep, research-based, and incredibly valuable. I've read many of them, and I respect the work immensely. But what I kept hearing from women, over and over again, was that something still felt missing. They didn't just want to learn how to communicate better or solve conflict faster (though those are important). What I came to realize was that they wanted to understand the energetic dance between masculine and feminine energies that makes love feel electric. They wanted to understand polarity.

And here's the truth: In today's world, the lines between men and women and masculine and feminine energies are more fluid than ever. Most of the women I work with are ambitious, successful, and deeply capable. They're leading teams, running companies, raising kids, managing homes—often doing it *all* with incredible grace. The old gender roles don't apply anymore. Both men and women are often working, leading, and providing. And while that's a beautiful evolution, it's also created brand-new challenges.

How do you create attraction—a magnetic pull between masculine and feminine energies—in a relationship where both people are "doing it all"? How do you stay connected to your feminine energy—not by shrinking, but by softening in a way that feels powerful, aligned, and safe? How do you invite your partner to rise into his masculine strength, without dimming your strength?

Those are the questions this book was built to answer. In today's rapidly evolving dating and relationship landscape, *Cracking the Man Code* taps into a cultural conversation that millions of women are having. It's the conversation I hear in coaching sessions, at seminars, in social DMs, even in quiet moments after a keynote. And it's more relevant now than ever before. Here are a few reasons why:

- **The relationship gender gap is growing.** Over 70 percent of divorces are initiated by women. Not because they don't value love, but because they feel emotionally unfulfilled—and they're done settling.
- **There's a masculinity crisis in modern relationships.** Many men feel unsure of what it means to be "a good man" today, and without a strong masculine presence, attraction and intimacy often begin to fade.
- **Relationship coaching is on the rise.** More women than ever are seeking guidance—not because they're failing, but because they're done wasting time. They want love that *works* and *lasts*.
- **The culture is shifting.** We're talking more openly about energy, polarity, feminine power, and emotional intelligence—and women are leading that conversation.

You are leading that conversation. If you've ever felt like you had to choose between being successful *or* soft, empowered *or* desired, strong *or* supported . . . this book is here to help you bridge that gap and create a love that honors *all* of who you are. Because at the end of the day, I believe we're here to love and be loved. That's the real game. The real treasure.

I was once asked, "If you were on your deathbed looking back at what defined your life, what would matter most?" For me, the answer was clear. It wouldn't be career accolades or viral videos. It would be my relationships. The love I gave. The love I shared. The love I helped others find.

That's why writing this book has been on my heart. Most of us were never handed a user manual for relationships. And unless you grew up with parents who modeled deep respect, great communication, and real emotional intimacy, you probably didn't get the clearest blueprint for lasting love. This book is here to change that. *Cracking the Man Code* was born out of a personal mission to help women who are ready for lasting, passionate, *real* love—and want to understand how to create it without losing themselves in the process.

While we all have both masculine and feminine energies within us, I'm writing this book primarily for women who want to be more grounded in their powerful feminine energy and attract a man who is more grounded in his authentic and healthy masculine energy. Why? Because that's who I most often get asked to serve—and the topic I know best. I use the traditional gender terms, "man" and "woman," but if those terms don't serve you, you can replace them with "masculine-grounded person" and "feminine-grounded person." The principles throughout this book are relevant to all genders and gender variations.

Now, if you're a woman, I know what you might be thinking: *Wait . . . this is a book for women, written by a man?* Fair question. But that's what makes this book your secret weapon. Most men aren't sitting around analyzing how they think, feel, and fall in love. But I do. It's literally my job. I've spent years immersed in this work, listening to men, coaching women, and studying what actually creates lasting, passionate connection—not just from textbooks or theory, but from lived, real-world experience. Think of this book as your behind-the-scenes pass. I'm handing you insights most women never get to hear, so you can stop second-guessing and start creating the partnership you truly want.

If you're in a same-sex relationship or identify outside of traditional gender roles, you'll still find tremendous value here. The principles of polarity apply to any dynamic where masculine and feminine energies are at play. If you're ready to experience love that's emotionally connected, spiritually aligned, and sexually alive . . . you're in the right place.

—— What This Book Is (and Is Not) ——

Now, you might be thinking, "Why isn't there a book helping men step up?"

Great question. I *do* believe men need to do the work. Big time. I also believe relationships are never 50/50. They're 100/100. If you want a thriving, lasting connection, both partners need to bring their best to the table. But here's the thing: you can't control what your man (or future man) does. You can only control *you*—how you show up, what you embody, and the energy you bring into your relationships. And the beautiful news is that when you shift, everything around you starts to shift, too. That's what this book gives you—the power to create momentum, without manipulation or self-abandonment.

The concepts in this book are not about changing who you are. They're not about playing games or pretending to be someone you're not. They are about stepping even more into your power with clarity, grace, and authenticity, while gaining a whole new understanding of the man in your life (or the one you're calling in).

Throughout my career, I've discovered that creating a lasting, passionate, connected relationship comes down to three essential phases:

Mindset—developing the belief systems that support the love you want to create.

Heartset—healing your past, loving yourself, and opening to new possibilities.

Skillset—learning the actual tools to build chemistry, connection, and powerful communication.

While mindset and heartset are essential (and we'll touch on them in this book), many incredible books have been written on those topics. This book, instead, is devoted to *skillset.*

Think of this book as your **relationship toolkit.** I'm going to reveal the secret drivers behind how men think, love, and communicate, so you can spark more romance, build a deeper emotional bond, and feel fully cherished in your relationship.

Cracking the Man Code is packed with transformative insights and practical tools you can start using *right away*. Inside you'll discover:

- The secret forces that drive attraction—and how to master them to spark undeniable chemistry.
- How to restore lost attraction and keep the spark alive for years to come.
- What fuels a man's love and devotion—and how to inspire more of it.
- How to speak a man's language so he truly hears and understands you.
- The secret to handling relationship conflict in a way that brings you closer, not apart.

Throughout this book, I'll share stories from women I've coached and couples I've worked with over the years. To protect privacy, names and details may be changed, but the transformations you'll read are real. And they're here to show you what's possible when you apply these tools.

— A Few Ground Rules Before We Start —

Focus on the Gold

Now, a quick heads-up: in order to talk about what men need, feel, fear, and crave most, I'm going to make some generalizations. Not because all men are the same, but because patterns are powerful—and when we understand the *common tendencies*, we gain insight that helps us connect on a deeper level.

So if you hear something that doesn't sound like your guy or your experience, don't worry. That's where your handy **How It Applies (HIA) Spotlight** comes in. Picture a miner's headlamp—beaming right onto the concepts that *do* land for you, while gently noticing the ones that don't. That way, instead of fixating on the exceptions, you stay focused on the gold.

Adjust Your "Offend-ability" Dial

Throughout this book, we'll talk about differences between masculine and feminine energy. This doesn't mean one is better than the other. Not even close. I believe, deeply, in the equal value of men and women and both masculine and feminine energies. But I also believe we're not designed to be carbon copies of each other. Our differences—when honored and understood—don't divide us. They *deepen* us. They help us create passion (that is, polarity—that dance of energies that makes love not just sweet, but magnetic!).

If a concept rubs you the wrong way, I invite you to stay open. You don't need to agree with everything in this book, but sometimes the biggest breakthroughs live on the other side of curiosity.

Tools, Not Rules

Rules can feel rigid, robotic, and outdated. (Like "Don't call him for three days or you'll look desperate." Come on.) Tools, on the other hand, are flexible. They're empowering. They work in real life—not just in theory. They give you the ability to respond to any situation with clarity, confidence, and grace.

That's what you'll find in these pages: not commandments, not gimmicks, just high-leverage tools that help you navigate love with more understanding and ease.

And not just romantic love. Here's the bonus: Once you understand men at this level, it transforms all your relationships. Your dad. Your brother. Your son. Your best friend. Even the guy handing you your latte at the coffee shop. When you shift your energy, people feel it and respond in powerful ways.

Ready to get started? Let's crack the man code.

Part One

Discovering Polarity

The One Thing That Changes Everything

Chapter One

The Twin Energies of Attraction

After retiring from the military, Tanya dove headfirst into the dating world, armed with confidence, curiosity, and a "get it done" mentality.

"I've been in combat. I can handle coffee dates and dating apps," she figured. But despite all her strength and smarts, love kept slipping through her fingers. She kept finding herself in the same exhausting pattern. She'd match with a guy, and if she didn't hear from him right away, she'd follow up. If a date needed to be set, she'd coordinate it. If the conversation fizzled, she'd throw in a joke, ask another question, keep it going. Basically, she did the work for both of them. And in return?

Ghosting. Flakiness. Mixed signals. Guys who loved chatting but never made a move. One guy even texted her daily for two months—sending emojis, voice notes, pictures of his dinner—but never once asked her to meet in person. And Tanya, being the mission-oriented, follow-through kind of woman she is, kept trying to "make it happen." Because that's what she was taught: If something matters, you work for it. You earn it.

But when it came to dating, all that effort just seemed to backfire. The more she pursued a man, the less he showed up. It wasn't just confusing—it was deflating. After yet another promising connection fizzled without explanation, Tanya tossed her phone on the couch, leaned forward with her elbows on her knees, and let out a long sigh. She stared at the floor, shaking her head slowly, and whispered, "What am I doing wrong?" There were no tears . . . yet. Just that quiet ache of a woman who's strong in every other area of life but starting to wonder if love was the one mission she'd never complete.

Sound familiar?

Maybe your experience looks like Tanya's, or maybe you're not in a relationship yet, but you're doing your best to stay sane in the wild world of modern dating. You match with a guy online. He's cute and clever, and he seems like he's got his life together. You message back and forth, and then . . . crickets. Or maybe you are in a relationship, but the emotional connection between you that once felt so alive now feels . . . distant. He's physically present but emotionally checked out. You try to connect by asking questions but get one-word answers or blank stares.

Maybe you've become the default CEO of your household. You plan the vacations, schedule the appointments, remember the birthdays, initiate the hard conversations . . . while he zones out to the TV or scrolls on his phone. You don't want to direct everything, but if you don't—who will?

Maybe you're in a relationship with a man who just won't lead. You ask, "Can we plan something fun together?" And he says, "Sure, what do you want to do?" And just like that, the ball is back in your court—and so is the mental load. You're left wondering, *What am I doing wrong?!*

That's exactly where Tanya found herself. Her mind filled with possibilities.

Maybe she was too much.

Maybe she wasn't enough.

Maybe love just wasn't in the cards for her.

All those thoughts echoed like a truth she was almost starting to believe. But none of those thoughts were true. Tanya wasn't broken, and love hadn't passed her by. She was just unknowingly leading in relationships with the same energy she used to command respect in every other area of her life—without realizing how it was affecting attraction.

— Everyday Magnetism —

There's an invisible current flowing beneath every romantic connection. A silent language that either pulls two people closer or quietly pushes them apart. And once you learn how to speak that language, everything changes.

That current is called polarity. Polarity happens when the twin energies of masculine and feminine come together; like the opposite poles of a magnet, they are irresistibly drawn to each other. Imagine holding two heavy, powerful magnets, one in each hand. When the positive and negative ends of these magnets are facing one another, you can feel each magnet pulling toward the other, as if they yearn to make contact with each other. If you allow the two magnets to get close enough, they snap together. Once connected, it takes a lot of energy to pull them apart. It's easier for these two magnets to be together than it is to stay apart. The natural energetic state of these two magnets is connection.

Now imagine flipping one of the magnets around so that both positive ends of the magnets are facing one another. Try to push them together. What happens?

The magnets repel one another. And not just a little bit. It's almost impossible to make these two magnets touch. It's as if they're judo masters, pushing one another to the side, deftly avoiding any possible contact. Why? Because the natural effect of two positive poles (or two negative poles) is to repel one another.

The same principle of magnetism applies in relationships. Our energy either builds romantic chemistry or repels it. This is one reason people find themselves in the friend zone. One of the main contributors to being "friend-zoned" is having the same type of energy as your potential love interest. This creates a lack of magnetism, and by extension a lack of attraction. Your potential partner is likely to see you as a fun buddy to hang out with.

If you feel like the high-quality man you're looking for is nowhere to be found—the kind of man who's emotionally available, grounded in his masculinity and purpose, and ready to show up for a real, lasting connection—then like a magnet, you must align your energy so that you have enough polarity to draw him in. The more aligned you are with your feminine energy, the more strongly you'll attract his masculine energy. And vice versa.

You may not even be aware of what energy you are giving out. It's not always easy to tell, because every human being has both masculine and feminine energy within them. You probably know men who express more feminine energy—nurturing, emotionally connected, intuitively receptive. And you probably know women who radiate more masculine energy—driven, decisive, goal-oriented. These energies aren't tied to your gender, and they're not fixed. How much of each energy you express in your life is influenced by a mix of factors, such as how you were raised, your role models, your life experiences, and even your own biology.

Although we have both energies within us, most of us have a core energy—a place that feels most natural to us. If you're not quite sure what your core energy is yet, don't worry—we'll dive deep into these energies in the next chapter (plus, at the end of this chapter, you'll be offered a masculine/feminine energy assessment).

What's both empowering and freeing is that *your energy is not static.* You can shift between masculine and feminine energies depending on the situation—and you probably already do. You might feel most at home in your masculine at work—leading meetings, hitting goals, solving problems. But in your relationship, you may crave softening into your feminine—being pursued, feeling cherished, and seeking emotional support. Or maybe your feminine shines when you're connecting with friends, sharing stories, and being open-hearted. But your masculine kicks in when you're making big decisions, going after a goal, or getting competitive—like when you're on the pickleball court, determined to take down that rival team and claim the win.

The goal isn't to *only* live in one energy forever—it's to *consciously* choose which one will best serve you in the moment. That awareness is your power.

I often describe masculine and feminine energy like a spectrum, with masculine on one end and feminine on the other. Instead of being locked into one spot, imagine you have a volume dial on your chest. You can dial up your feminine energy when you want to feel more radiant, receptive, and connected, or dial up your masculine when it's time to get things done, take charge, or protect what matters most.

The more skilled you become at adjusting that dial, the more magnetic and fulfilled you'll feel—not just in dating or love, but in every area of your life.

— Making Room for the Feminine —

I'm going to assume you're here because you're looking to dial up your feminine energy when it comes to your relationships (even if you don't yet realize that). Now, you might hear "feminine energy" and think, *Awesome! I'm ready to hone my skills!* Or you may roll your eyes at those words because you think of the simplistic and clichéd expressions of femininity from the past: wearing frilly dresses, always putting on a full face of makeup, talking in a syrupy-sweet, high-pitched voice, and, worst of all, completely giving up your power or any sort of control in your life, especially in your relationships. The thought of "being more feminine" makes you want to vomit because you're a smart, successful badass and you shouldn't have to change who you are just to attract some guy into your life. *Right?*

I totally get it. Which is why I'm committed to calling out the old, outdated beliefs about what it means to be feminine, pulling them out by the roots, and setting them ablaze. Hear me when I say, you do *not* have to give up your power to become more feminine. Stepping into your feminine energy will require claiming even more of your authentic power. So, rest easy.

To have a successful relationship you don't have to become someone you're not. But you may benefit from shifting some behaviors or adjusting some habits if you want to activate more of your feminine power, just like improving your physical health requires making some changes (such as eating healthier foods and exercising).

Take my client, Vanessa, for example. Vanessa was a successful businesswoman in her mid-thirties who radiated intelligence, confidence, and some serious attitude. She sat in the front row of my Cracking the Man Code seminar. As I looked out over the audience, I immediately noticed her arms folded tight across her chest, her crossed legs, lowered brows, and narrowed eyes. Everything about her screamed, "Okay, hotshot, try to tell me something I don't already know."

When I reached the topic of masculine and feminine energy and began to explain how these energies work together, I saw her mouth twist into a smirk as her hand shot up. Experience told me that she probably didn't have a question but was preparing to lead the "feminine energy is horsesh*t!" chant. I called on her, a bit hesitantly, aware I was about to open a can of worms.

Sure enough, Vanessa said, "I think feminine energy is a bunch of crap. I'm an educated, powerful, successful woman. I own my own business. Why should I have to change myself to attract a powerful man? I should just be able to be myself." A wave of nodding heads rippled through the crowd.

"You're absolutely right, Vanessa," I replied. "You don't have to change who you are. You don't have to stop being a powerful woman. You don't have to stop leading a successful business. Just let me ask you this: How is your current love-life strategy working for you?"

She frowned and looked down. "Well, not great," she muttered. Then she lifted her head and, looking me straight in the eye, said, "But men should be able to love me as I am, and not be intimidated by my success."

"Again, you're right," I told her. "However, I don't believe it's solely intimidation that's causing your 'not great' results. If you're looking for a successful, masculine man, there are things you can do as a powerful, strong woman to help ignite his attraction to you. But . . . it requires being willing to try something different if you want different results."

Vanessa's face softened, and she unfolded her arms. What followed was a frank and vulnerable discussion of what happened on Vanessa's dates. As she talked, what stood out to me was a lack of receptivity on her part, which came across as competitiveness. She was so intent on proving that she was a smart, successful, capable woman that she left little room to receive what her date was trying to contribute. I suggested she try letting her date give to her by accepting graciously.

"Notice the moments when your date tries to provide something for you, and then open up and receive it," I said.

She was a bit skeptical but agreed to give it a try. "I've got nothing to lose," she said. A week later, I got a message from Vanessa saying, "Oh my gosh, it worked!" She described going on a first date with a man named Adam. They were going to meet at a coffee shop they both liked at 10 AM. A few minutes before ten, Vanessa drove up to the gate to pay for parking in the lot across the street. Adam pulled in right behind Vanessa. Recognizing her from her photos, and seeing she was about to pay, he jumped out of his car, ran up to the gate, and offered to pay for her parking.

Vanessa's first instinct was to decline. She wanted Adam to know that she made her own money and that she could afford to pay for her own parking. But just as the word "no" was forming on her lips, she paused. Remembering our conversation at the seminar, she thought to herself, *Okay, let me try receiving.*

"You know what?" she answered. "That would be nice. Thank you!" Vanessa said she could see Adam's shoulders broaden and his face brighten as he paid for her parking. As the gate arm lifted and she drove through, Adam looked as if he had just slain a dragon for her. Vanessa smiled to herself, seeing how big an emotional reward he received from such a small action.

That first date sparked an incredible romance filled with passion and partnership—one in which Vanessa never had to give up her integrity or power. The couple married two years later and are still happily wed.

Vanessa's story is not unique. I've seen hundreds of powerful, strong, successful women continue to be who they are while embracing their feminine side—an energy they'd either shut down or never fully explored.

One of those women was Tanya, from earlier in this chapter—the former military commander who'd spent years putting in the effort, making the plans, and carrying the emotional weight in every dating situation, only to be left on read, let down, or ghosted altogether. For a long time, Tanya assumed it was her. That maybe she was asking too much. That maybe love just wasn't in the cards. But everything changed when she began exploring masculine and feminine energy. When she realized she had been filling the entire space in the connection—initiating, leading, solving, proving—she decided to try something new.

She didn't stop being powerful. She didn't give up her strength. She simply made a conscious choice to stop over-functioning in the masculine. She paused. She softened. She let herself receive, instead of doing all the leading. And in that space, something beautiful happened. A man showed up who wanted to lead. Who had a plan. Who pursued her with consistency and clarity. And this time, Tanya didn't meet his effort with control or skepticism. She received it.

Today, Tanya is with a man who sees her fully—strength and softness, grit and grace. A partner who honors her feminine energy, not despite her power, but because of it. When she stopped doing the work for him, he finally had the space to step up. That's the power of polarity. That's the magnetism we're about to dive even deeper into.

In the next chapter, we'll break down the seven key characteristics of masculine and feminine energy—and show you exactly how to embody the energy that creates real, lasting attraction in your love life.

GIFT BOX

Curious about where you naturally land on the masculine-feminine spectrum? Take this quick, easy quiz to uncover your dominant energy and gain key insights into how it's shaping your love life.

Chapter Two

Masculine and Feminine

— A Tale of Two Energies —

As I mentioned earlier, I've been a romantic for as long as I can remember. While other kids dreamed of touchdowns or spacewalks, I was daydreaming about love—long before I could even spell "relationship." At eight years old, I wasn't just playing tag on the playground; I was picking out which girl I might marry.

By junior high, I decided it was time to take things up a notch and get serious about my "love education." Naturally, I turned to the best expert I knew—my big sister, Jennifer. She was two and a half years older, a magnet for attention, and, in my eyes, a certified boy-whisperer.

She became my coach, prepping me for the Dating Olympics. She was going to teach me how to be "more attractive." First up was grooming—starting with the merciless elimination of my adolescent unibrow. (Let's just say tweezers became my new frenemy.) Next was my hair.

She wielded a curling iron with the precision of a sushi chef, shellacking my bangs into the ideal '90s heartthrob wave. Add in a gallon of hairspray, and I was practically weatherproof.

Then she gave me fashion tips, which I followed once—and only once—when she convinced me that white button-downs, pegged jeans, and sockless penny loafers would drive the girls wild. What it actually did was make me the centerpiece of lunchtime jokes for a week. But hey, I was all in.

By the time I hit twenty, I had the playbook down. I'd learned how to create attraction the way she had—indirectly, subtly, by encouraging my love interests to pursue me. I knew how to give just the right smile, make the right eye contact, and steer a conversation so the girl was asking for my number. It worked . . . sort of. It worked at getting attention. It worked at making me feel safe—less risk of rejection when I wasn't the one taking the lead. But what I didn't realize at the time was that my sister's approach—brilliant as it was—was rooted in feminine energy. Without knowing it, I had adopted that energy in how I approached dating. Which meant the kind of women who were drawn to me were mostly in their masculine energy—driven, decisive, take-charge types.

The problem? I'm a masculine-energy guy at my core. So eventually, I'd shift back into my natural energy, and the polarity would vanish. Suddenly, it felt like we were both trying to drive the same car at the same time. Relationships fizzled. Or flopped. Or flat-out exploded in miscommunication and unmet needs.

And I didn't have a clue *why*, until, when in my late twenties, I discovered what you're learning right now.

Understanding masculine and feminine energy transformed my love life. I've also watched it transform the lives of thousands of women I've coached over the years. I'll never forget the moment one of my clients—a former police officer—said to me on a call:

"Mat, I've spent twenty years busting bad guys, and I've got two older brothers. I was raised by a single dad. I know how to take charge. But this whole *feminine energy* thing? I don't even know what that looks like. Am I a lost cause?"

Not even close.

I told her what I'll tell you now: it doesn't matter how you were raised or what role you've played in the world. Feminine energy isn't about being soft or passive. It's about reconnecting to your natural magnetic power.

It's not something you "perform." It's something you *embody*. The first step is understanding the core qualities of both masculine and feminine energy, and how these forces interact to create real attraction. To give you a head start, I've put together a simple, clear breakdown of the most common attributes of each energy.

This is a good time to remember the "tools" over "rules" principle. Remember, rules always have an exception. Tools, on the other hand, can be used in many different circumstances to serve you in creating the results you want. So consider this list below a nice tool to help you understand the complementary expressions of masculine and feminine energies.

Feminine Energy Is:	Masculine Energy Is:
• Receiving	• Providing
• Nurturing	• Protecting
• Collaborative	• Competitive
• Heart/Feeling	• Head/Thinking
• Allowing/Accommodating	• Directing/Asserting
• Beautifying	• Practical
• "Pulling" (Invitational)	• "Pursuing"

In a moment, we'll unpack specific examples of how each of these qualities show up in relationships. But first, understand that the list above represents healthy, productive expressions of masculine and feminine energies. There are also dysfunctional or toxic expressions of masculine and feminine energy, which I've put into the following list.

Toxic Feminine Energy Is:	*Toxic* Masculine Energy Is:
• Weak • Submissive • Passive • Self-effacing • Manipulative • Helpless • Needy	• Threatening • Dominating • Aggressive • Arrogant • Controlling • Selfish • Detached

It's no wonder that some people have such a negative reaction to the idea of masculine and feminine energy. It's a shame that so many of us have had to experience these toxic examples at some point in our lives.

These dysfunctional qualities emerge when the masculine or feminine energies are based in fear rather than love: fear of loss, fear of betrayal, fear of getting hurt. When fear is in the driver's seat, relationships become constricting, destructive, and painful.

On the other hand, if we're able to harness the healthy versions of feminine or masculine energies—energies sourced in love—then we build one another up; the relationship feels more expansive and becomes life-giving. With that in mind, let's dive into the healthy qualities of masculine and feminine energy and explore what they look like inside of relationships.

— Receiving Versus Providing —

Masculine energy wants to provide. It can be something small—like paying for parking on a date, offering a jacket if you're cold, or pulling out your chair—or a larger gesture, like whisking you away on a romantic getaway weekend, or taking the day off to care for you when you're sick. No matter the scale, masculine men are hardwired to want to deliver you happiness.

The complementary energy to providing is the willingness to receive.

Like beautiful open arms extended wide, feminine energy takes in what the masculine provides, validating the masculine's efforts. A woman expressing a lot of feminine energy is a gracious and appreciative receiver, in no way "less than" the provider, but an equal partner in the dance of give and receive.

This is often easier said than done. When starting our relationship coaching programs, many women are very comfortable providing for others but struggle with their willingness to receive. Many have either been let down in the past by other partners, or they don't want to be a "burden" or "too needy." Others have spent years being the sole provider for their kids, so giving has become an ingrained habit. Still others are afraid of feeling obligated to anyone.

The ability to receive is like a muscle. When you practice receiving by using the effective techniques (more about that in chapter four), your "receiving muscle" gets stronger and something amazing happens: not only do you create a wonderful experience for your masculine man to be able to give to you, but your own self-esteem grows as well.

That might seem strange, but here's how it works. Each time you joyfully receive from another person, you send a message to your subconscious mind that you are worthy of their love and attention—and that your desires matter. Conversely, when you reject someone's attempt to give from their heart, you send the signal to your subconscious that you're not worthy of their love. The more you allow yourself to receive, the more your heart opens, flinging wide the door to experience deeper love in your life.

A client of mine named Sabrina shared with me the impact her newfound receptivity skills had on her and on her relationship. One night, Sabrina's boyfriend called on his way home from work asking if she'd like him to swing by a restaurant and bring her some takeout. She was hungry and felt a wave of gratitude at his offer. But immediately, she felt her old patterns rise in resistance. She thought, *C'mon, Sabrina, you can make your own food. Don't be needy and make him go out of his way just for you.*

Firmly interrupting those old limiting ideas, she reminded herself that receiving a gift actually honors the giver, and that she was worthy of his effort to love her this way. Overriding the part of her that didn't want to be a burden, she simply said, "Yes, that'd be great."

When he arrived, carrying a bag of delicious-smelling Thai food, Sabrina hugged him and thanked him for the meal. Stepping back, she saw a huge smile on his face and his eyes shining with pleasure and pride. In that moment, she truly understood that receiving was not taking something from him but rather giving something to him. By saying yes, she'd given him the opportunity to provide—an experience he and his masculine energy deeply desire. Receiving in this way had also allowed her to honor her own value, which was every bit as enjoyable and nourishing—if not more so—as her perfectly spiced dinner of pad thai.

One final thought on the topic of receiving: often my clients ask, "What if I make more money than he does, or what if I'm the sole financial provider for us both—does that kill the polarity?" The answer: It doesn't have to. As long as you find ways for him to provide you with what you want, he's utilizing his masculine energy. These can be simple things like a date night, a fun outing, opening a jar of jam, or pleasing you in the bedroom. Finances are just one aspect of the relationship; there are literally thousands of other ways for you to receive from your partner.

— Nurturing Versus Protecting —

Nurturing and protecting are contrasting qualities, yet both are expressions of the same feeling of "I love you and care about you."

Protecting, like providing, has been the aim of the masculine for thousands of years. People with masculine energy are compelled to protect—to fight wars, defend the home, and do everything they can to shield those they love from harm.

A man with healthy masculine energy is determined to protect you from any and all threats. Whether he walks on the traffic side of the sidewalk, rotates the tires on your car to prevent an accident, or stands between you and an armed gunman, he wants to ensure that you're safe. And not just that. He wants you to *feel* safe in his presence. In the quiet moments, when it's just the two of you, your feeling safe enough to relax is a beautiful validation that he is doing a good job as your man.

Feminine energy, on the other hand, loves to nurture. Nurturing is not about protecting against danger, but rather helping a loved one thrive, and it comes in many forms. The feminine loves to care for those around them, and make sure everyone has what they need to succeed. For example, a parent, whether male or female, is tapping into their feminine energy when they make sure the kids have enough food in their little bellies, the right shoes on their feet before they run outside, or the proper blankets at night to keep them warm.

A person in nurturing mode receives joy from anticipating the wants and needs of their partner, whether that's preparing a meal that nourishes the body and soul, or creating an environment that helps your partner relax and feel at home. In whatever way you choose to express it, the practice of nurturing connects you to your feminine energy.

As you can imagine, sometimes the man will play the nurturer role and the woman the protector role. However, if two people in a relationship both play the same role, both nurturers or both protectors, too much of the time—it can be easy to lose the polarity between them.

Creating lasting attraction requires awareness of these dynamics and the ability to consciously choose when necessary to step into your masculine or feminine energy. There's no right or wrong here, *but* if you aren't intentional about creating polarity, you'll wind up with a good friendship rather than an extraordinary romance.

This is a common problem for many of the single moms I work with. Because they're constantly protecting (and providing for) their kids, they're often stuck in their masculine energy, repelling the type of masculine man they say they want.

Although it's a challenging spot to be in, the good news is that as you master the masculine–feminine spectrum, you'll be able to easily move from the masculine to the feminine with ease and grace.

— Collaborative Versus Competitive —

Feminine energy loves to work with others for a common objective; more valuable than accomplishment is the feeling of connection that's created along the way. The feminine wants to make sure everyone is involved in a project, that no one gets left out, and, even more importantly, that everyone has a good time. At a dinner party, it's feminine energy that wants to make sure everyone has a chance to share their experiences, stories, or opinions, and when selecting a restaurant, that everyone is on board with the location.

The feminine is tuned in to the emotional state of others and strives to create harmony. When there's friction in a relationship, the feminine feels a strong urge to reconcile because it receives validation through connection.

Conversely, people with masculine energy receive validation through competition. They love achieving goals and competing with others. The masculine asks, "What game are we playing and how can I win?" If there's no obvious game to be played, give someone with a lot of masculine energy a few minutes and they'll invent a game and invite you to join. Whether it's playing chess, skipping rocks across a pond, racing up a hill, or throwing crumpled pieces of paper into a wastebasket carefully placed fifteen feet across the room, the masculine gets a surge of energy when competing against a worthy adversary. Those with masculine energy especially love dates that have anything to do with competition, games, or action, like bowling, playing pool, biking, golfing, hiking, surfing, rock climbing, escape rooms, and so on. Any chance to win and the masculine is all in.

Yet more than anything, a healthy masculine man wants to know he's won your heart. He longs to feel special, knowing you've chosen him over all other men. He deeply desires to feel significant in your eyes and that he's earned the right to stand by your side and share your life.

You can always tell whether you're expressing masculine energy or feminine energy by identifying your priorities in an activity: Are you more invested in competing? Or connecting?

— Heart/Feeling Versus Head/Thinking —

Which part of your body are you more connected to throughout the day—your head or your heart? Do you tend to spend most of your day in your head, thinking, strategizing, and analyzing? Or are you more connected to your heart space, feeling your way through the day? Your answers to these questions will let you know whether you're in your masculine or your feminine energy.

Masculine energy is expressed through the head and is associated with our thinking. It is future-oriented. The masculine wants to set goals, envision the future, create strategies, solve problems, and make plans for your time together.

Feminine energy, on the other hand, is heart-centered and connected to the body. When you're in touch with your feelings and are aware of your physical and emotional state, you're plugged in to your feminine energy. This strong connection with the heart and body is why the feminine is more present-oriented. The only time you can feel your feelings or notice your physical experience is in the moment happening *right now*. In fact, one of the easiest ways to access the present moment—and by extension your feminine energy—is to bring your awareness to your body. Whether you're dancing, singing, creating art, or making love, there is nothing more alluring to the masculine than a woman who is connected to her heart-space and present in her body, deeply feeling the joy of the moment.

An illustration of these qualities in action comes from Catherine, a woman who began exploring these Cracking the Man Code ideas. Catherine sent me this story describing her experience of being *Heart/Feeling* oriented in contrast to her boyfriend's more masculine *Head/Thinking* approach:

Catherine

A few years ago, my boyfriend David and I took a trip to Hawaii to escape the Idaho winter and enjoy some quality time together. It was a well-planned vacation—from the tour guide we hired to take us on the Road to Hana, to the beachside Airbnb (with kitchen, to save on meals). After landing in Maui, David settled into the driver's seat of the rental car, slid the car into gear, and began driving.

I rolled down the window, basking in the sunshine and breathing in the delicious scent of tropical flowers and salt water, as David briskly listed the itinerary: first to the grocery store, where we'd stock up on fresh fish, fruit, and water. Next to the Airbnb, to get checked in and unpack. Then to the dive shop where we'd rent snorkels, fins, and bodyboards. His get-it-done energy, while definitely efficient, felt at odds with our surroundings.

I reached across the center console, slid my hand into his, and said, "The beach is right there, baby. Will you take me there first?" Surprise and amusement washed over his face. He laughed as though to say, "Oh, right! Duh!" I watched him mentally adjust "the mission" as he drove us to Charley Young Beach. We walked down the sandy slope to the water's edge, took off our shoes, and immediately melted into "Maui Time."

Within seconds, the powdery sand coated our feet, invading every nook and cranny of our newly liberated toes. The warm ocean breeze swayed the fronds above our heads, casting us into shade, and light, and shade again.

As the crystalline blue, bathwater-warm waves swirled around our knees, soaking our airplane clothes, I laughed with delight. David leaned down, kissed me, and said, "What were we supposed to be doing?"

As you can see, one of the great gifts the feminine gives to the masculine is to help him get out of his head, drop into his heart, and experience the richness of the here and now.

— Allowing Versus Directing —

Allowing can be one of the hardest feminine attributes to embody, especially if you're used to being in your masculine directive energy. Managers, entrepreneurs, and executives are richly rewarded for using their masculine energy to direct the outcomes they want.

Switching to the feminine energy of allowing means being willing to loosen your grip on control and let go—empowering others to bring forward their best. Allowing requires that you trust others, and that you believe in their capability to deliver what you want, without trying to control their every step. What's interesting is that the best leaders have learned to harness both their feminine and masculine energies, directing when needed, but also trusting their teams enough to allow them to deliver the result without overseeing every step in the process.

In a romantic relationship, the feminine *allows* the masculine to serve and provide what the feminine desires—the way my wife, Irene, did on our first date, when she leaned back, allowing me to step up and make the plan for our evening together. This kind of allowing requires the feminine to trust and believe in the masculine's ability to create the desired outcome—without micromanaging or second-guessing.

This trust is something the masculine craves intensely. Allowing is not passivity or helplessness on the part of the feminine. To allow the masculine to direct requires poise, strength, and confidence.

— Beautifying Versus Practical —

The feminine loves to add beauty and color to the world. Whether enhancing a house with artwork, photos, plants, flowers, candles, and throws, or selecting a wardrobe of beautiful clothes in all different tones and textures, the feminine receives joy through beautification.

In contrast, the masculine loves practicality. Once a house has a couch, a bed, a fridge, and a big-screen TV with surround sound, the masculine is happy to stop decorating. The masculine asks:

"Do we really need all these pillows on the bed when we only sleep with one of them?"

"Chargers are plates we never eat on? And you want them because . . . ?"

"What do you mean you don't like this bracelet? It's got a compass, paracord, and knife all in one."

"These pants double as shorts when you unzip the knees—cool, right?!"

Being practical includes a quest for efficiency. It's the masculine that thinks, *Shampoo and conditioner in one bottle? Awesome!* Or tries to carry up too many grocery bags at once because he doesn't want to make multiple trips from the car to the house (inevitably dropping the corn chips and bagels on the ground). The masculine shoves giant piles of clothes into the washing machine, packing them in as tightly as possible because doing one load of laundry is better than having to do two.

Yet, even with these differences, the healthy masculine man truly appreciates the magical ability of the feminine to turn a house into a home, as she breathes warmth, light, color, and beauty into their lives.

Pulling Energy Versus Pursuing Energy

The difference between pulling energy and pursuing energy is illustrated by the following scenario:

Imagine a woman, out with her friends at a party, sending a warm gaze and friendly smile to a man she finds attractive across the room. It's clear she wants to talk to him, but she stays where she is, allowing the distance between them to create a vacuum, pulling him toward her. This indirect invitation compels the man to cross the room and approach the woman if he wants to talk with her.

Of course, today, both men and women can do the approaching. But as we've learned, the person who is actively pursuing someone else is the one in their masculine energy. The feminine uses the power of pulling energy to help generate attraction.

The feminine sends signals like playful eye contact, subtle smiles, or body language to call over the masculine. To try to fulfill the desires of the feminine, the masculine pursues and fills the space created by the feminine.

The feminine is a master at creating desire. The masculine focuses on fulfilling desire. Great lovers are able to access both their feminine and masculine energies at different times, igniting desires and fulfilling desires, creating a powerful and sexy spectrum of experience.

Understanding the previous concepts gives you a huge head start when it comes to interacting with feminine and masculine energies. You can see how these energies fit together like two great ballroom dancers whirling and floating across the dance floor in perfect synchrony. When done well, this dance is a marvelous sight and an even more extraordinary experience.

But as you know, the dance of a relationship isn't always smooth. There will be times when we're out of sync with one another, and it seems as if our partner is moving to a beat all their own—one that makes no sense to us. These painful disconnects are often rooted in our differing instincts, which we'll explore in the next chapter.

When you understand the intricacies of your man's inner world and his natural masculine instincts—and he understands your inner world and natural feminine instincts—you both vastly improve your ability to get back in sync quickly.

GIFT BOX

Want a special pocket-sized cheat sheet of these masculine and feminine qualities? Download it here.

Chapter Three

Befriending His Inner Caveman

"Honey, have you seen the pickles?" Kevin called out to his wife as he bent over to peer at the contents of the open fridge like Sherlock Holmes searching for clues.

"They're on the second shelf," Megan called back from the adjacent family room, where she sat reading.

"No, they're not," Kevin said confidently. "I'm looking right at the second shelf, and there are no pickles."

Sighing, Megan closed her book and walked over to the fridge. She reached over Kevin's right shoulder, moved the mayonnaise two inches to the left, and pulled out the jar of Vlasic Kosher Dill Spear Pickles.

"I couldn't . . . they were . . . it wasn't . . ." Kevin stammered. Then, taking the jar from her, he smiled sheepishly. "Thanks, babe," he said.

"Uh-huh. Anything else you need help finding?" she said, giving him a peck on the cheek and a pat on the butt before she turned to go back to the family room.

Kevin blew out a breath. "Nope," he said, "that'll do it. I'm just gonna go make my sandwich now . . ."

Sound familiar?

Chances are you've had a "male refrigerator blindness" moment like this with a man in your life. Or, perhaps you've had moments when getting him to share his thoughts and feelings is like pulling teeth, especially when he's stressed. Then there's the way he tries to jump in and fix your problems, when what you really want is for him to just listen and be there for you. Or, how about the way he bristles when you try to give him helpful advice while he's working on a task. Or, insert your own variation of *Why can't he find the damn pickles?!*

If you can relate to any of these scenarios, you know how frustrating it is when you're not on the same page with your man. When you're thinking, *This is so obvious. Why can't he just see things the way I see them?* Or, *Why do I have to tell him what I need? He should just know.*

It's human nature to expect others to experience and perceive the world the way we do, at least for the most part. The man in your life should just "get it," like your girlfriends do. But interpreting men's actions through the lens of what it would mean if you, or another woman, did the same thing, can leave you feeling frustrated or, at a minimum, confused. I once heard relationship expert and best-selling author Alison Armstrong describe the disconnect this way: "Women look at men and see hairy, misbehaving women." So even though there's a lot about men and women that's the same, it's the small but important differences in our perceptions, innermost desires, and approach to relationships that can lead to unnecessary struggles.

One of the best ways to build a stronger connection with men is to gain a better understanding of these differences. Why do so many men think the way they do? What are their deeper internal motivations? In the following pages, we're going to explore these differences in detail so that you can see the gaps for what they are and build the bridge that leads to a more profound connection.

But before we take a deep dive into exploring our differences and where they came from, let me warn you—we're about to enter "Generalization-ville," where I'll be making generalizations to which there are *always* exceptions. If you want to get the most out of this section, now's the time to turn on your "How It Applies Spotlight" I mentioned in the introduction.

As you read through the following examples, look for the experiences you relate to, and leave the rest. This will help you understand your relationships better and empower you to give and receive love in an even deeper way.

HIA Spotlight on? Good! Let's begin.

— Basic Instinct: Mog and Grog Style —

As I was trying to better understand my own natural masculine instincts and the instincts of the women I dated, exploring the history of our hunter/gatherer ancestors was extremely useful in helping me grasp some of these differences.

To aid us in becoming more accepting and understanding of the varied ways the masculine and feminine operate, let's jump inside an imaginary time machine and travel back, back, back, several hundred thousand years and check out a day in the life of our cave ancestors, Grog and Mog.

Meet Caveman Grog, aka Mr. Hunter. Grog, ruggedly handsome—and likely very hairy—had one primary job: to hunt. And hunt bravely he did, venturing out with his band of cave-buddies on the all-important mission of catching lunch.

The more successful Grog was at his job, the greater the chance his family had of surviving. Which is why our cave-hubby Grog took his job of providing for his family very seriously. He got exceptionally good at spending hours at a time not speaking more than a word or two to his fellow hunters as they tracked their prey. Why? Because too much talking scared away lunch, of course. As a result, our prehistoric forefathers became masters at communicating only what information was absolutely necessary and being comfortable with very loooooong stretches of silence.

Perhaps you can relate. Ever ask your man, "How was your day, honey?" and he gave you the very eloquent response, "Good"? Or found yourself frustrated because your man neglected to share the details about plans he'd made? That's your man's inner Grog at work.

Grog also learned that efficiency matters. He had to carefully weigh his actions—would an all-out chase up a hill after that gazelle be worth the energy spent? He knew burning more calories than he would consume defeated the whole purpose of hunting and could even be fatal. "Do only what's necessary for the result. And accomplish the goal as quickly as possible" became Grog's hunting mantra. This could be one reason why your masculine man loves shortcuts and will choose to make a beeline toward a store—tromping through bushes and walking around barriers—rather than stay on the paved sidewalk that will take thirty seconds longer. Or why he texts instead of calls. If he can get to the goal quicker and with less energy, he will.

Grog developed the superb ability to ignore anything unrelated to his mission, because one small distraction could sabotage the all-important job of feeding his family. Many men today have inherited this same "mission-focused" way of being, which is why he just *has to* finish the task he's engaged in before he can respond to you. Or why, on his way to the bedroom to get his jacket, he steps over the kids' toys instead of picking them up. This mission-focused—one thing at a time without seeing the rest—approach to life can be incomprehensible to a woman.

Since Grog is only half the story, let's meet his lovely mate, Mog—aka Mrs. Gatherer. Understanding her instincts and responsibilities can give us insight into how the feminine operates.

Mog's job was multifaceted. Her dual role as a mother and gatherer demanded that she always be aware of her surroundings. When she wasn't out gathering with the other cavewomen in her group, she was back at home keeping one eye on the cooking fire, her other eye on her cave-babies, and somehow also watching out for predators on the prowl—all while sharing with the other cavewomen the exact details and location of the new fruit tree she'd discovered.

Modern-day women often have that same 360-degree awareness of everything going on around them, and a strong drive to take care of *all* of it. Instead of being mission-focused, women have an "everything-matters focus." For example, if you're on the way to get your jacket from the bedroom and see the kids' toys lying on the floor, you feel compelled to stop and put them away. Or, just as you're trying to leave the house, the kitchen counters demand to be wiped; the dishes say, "Put me away;" and the couch cushions absolutely have to be straightened. The downside of noticing everything is that it can be exhausting.

Another talent that helped Mog thrive was learning to work in perfect concert with the other cavewomen. The better the cavewomen cooperated, passed tasks back and forth, and helped each other—like members of a precision drill team—the greater their families' health and happiness. As a result, Mog became highly skilled at communicating with other women to get her important work done. She learned to notice the small early signs of frustration and friction, so she could steer the relationships back to a place of togetherness.

Getting along with the other cavewomen didn't just make for a nice cave-experience, it was a matter of survival. For a cavewoman, getting shunned from the community was the worst possible punishment, because banishment would almost certainly be fatal. Though it's no longer a matter of life and death, many women today feel that same deeply rooted need to be accepted by the group and a strong aversion to displeasing others.

For Grog, the opposite was true. Instead of his ability to fit into the group, Grog's status and security in the tribe was based on his willingness to stand up to those who would challenge him or threaten his family. He needed to prove that he was a worthy warrior capable of protecting—and providing for—all those who relied on him. This strong need to provide and protect remains an important priority for masculine men today.

For hundreds of thousands of years, this was how we humans

survived. Remnants of these behaviors influence our modern-day choices and actions in countless ways, which we'll explore next.

Fast-Forward: Grog and Mog's Gifts to Us

Bits of Mog and Grog show up in our instinctual behaviors and our physical senses. For example, when dining out, does your man like to sit on the side of the table facing the entrance of the restaurant? Most men do. This preference could be the result of thousands of years of conditioning, from the time when Grog sat facing the entrance of the cave, ready to protect against possible threats.

Or, as a woman, when telling a story do you like to give every last juicy detail to your friends? If so, this conversation style could be influenced by the thousands of years Mog spent giving her sister cavewomen the exact coordinates and every detail she could think of to help them reach the berry patch she had just discovered.

Another fascinating difference in men's and women's instinctual behaviors shows up in how we shop. For most masculine men, shopping is a hunting expedition with a clear mission: bring home the desired item as quickly and efficiently as possible. The fewer stores visited, the less energy expended, the less time it takes—the better.

For many women, the experience is quite different. If you're more interested in checking out all the options available before selecting the item you want, then you're operating more like Mog the gatherer. The feminine instinct is to look at everything on a rack or shelf, often visiting multiple stores, before making a purchase. What's more, most women enjoy the process, especially if it's done in the company of other women—a holdover from the days when cavewomen ventured out in groups looking for the optimal food to feed their families.

My wife, Irene, is a gatherer extraordinaire, which I sometimes forget when pursuing my own hunter agenda. Once, just a few weeks after our first child was born, I set out with Irene to buy a birthday present for my sister. Irene had been mostly homebound for a month, but we'd arranged for Grandma to babysit for a rare and coveted couple of hours so we could go shopping at one of Irene's favorite clothing stores, Charming Charlie. This was the first outing without our baby strapped to mama's hip, and Irene was feeling the joy of two full hours of freedom.

As soon as we stepped into the store, Irene began browsing and within a few minutes called me over to see a stylish top she'd found. I took one look and said, "This is the one, honey! My sister will love it."

I whisked it out of her hands and went straight over to the cash register to pay for it. Five minutes later, we were out the door and headed back to the car. I was stoked. "Irene, that was fantastic! We got that present in ten minutes flat! We are awesome!"

You can imagine my shock when, right there in the parking lot, tears began to stream down Irene's face, as she told me, "I-I-I wanted t-to sho-o-o-p." Seeing how upset she was, I immediately took her in my arms to comfort her. When she finished crying, she said, "Oh, Mat, I've been looking forward to spending some time at Charming Charlie for days . . ."

I apologized, offering to go back into the store so she could finish looking around.

She shook her head. "Thanks, but it's not the same," she said. "You've already bought the present."

My win wasn't a win for her at all. Lesson learned! Understanding the evolutionary roots of our different desires can help you to accept, honor, and anticipate your partner's wants and needs.

— Making Sense of Our Senses —

Our years as hunters and gatherers also contributed to actual physical/biological differences in our sense organs and how they function. Some of the conflicts and misunderstandings between men and women can be traced to the fact that we literally perceive the world differently. As we explore these differences one at a time, notice if you can relate to any of them in your relationships.

Vision

Over millennia, our eyesight evolved to support our roles as either hunters or gatherers. For example, most women can distinguish subtle differences in color far better than men can.[1] That's because, on average, women have more cones in the backs of their eyes than men do. (Cones are the cells in the retina that allow us to see color.[2])

Distinguishing between the slightly different hues of poisonous and nonpoisonous berries was a pretty handy skill for the gatherer, and it explains why, today, women use words like "mauve," "lavender," "plum," and "eggplant" to describe colors a man will simply call "purple."

I've run into this myself. One year, looking to buy my mother a birthday present, I called a client of mine who owned a business making gorgeous hand-knitted shawls and told her I wanted a white one.

"Well, we have pearl, powder, porcelain, eggshell, and ivory. Which color do you want?" she asked.

My brain froze. "*Uuuuhhhh,* which one is closest to white?"

My client had a bit of a laugh at that, but after some discussion, she helped me pick a color. It was my turn to laugh when my mother opened her gift and, turning toward me with a delighted smile, said, "Oh, Mat, it's perfect. I love eggshell!"

In addition to a refined color sense, most women also have better peripheral vision than men—another crucial survival advantage for a gatherer.[3] The cavewoman out looking for food in the field needed good peripheral vision to spot predators in time to avoid being a tasty snack, and thereby survive to pass that trait down to her daughter, who passed it on to her daughter, and so on.

Men, on the other hand, have better detection of movement and long-range detail, allowing them to spot approaching predators well in advance and see buffalo and other prey on the top of the next hill.[4] This could be a factor in men not being able to find nonmoving items—like pickle jars—that are right in front of them! I once had a client ask me if this is why men get caught checking out women more than women get caught checking out men, even though *both* sexes do a healthy amount of checking each other out. I told my client, yes! We men have to turn our heads to get a straight-on look at a woman we find attractive passing by.

As a woman, you can be more covert. When a sexy man walks in the room, you can continue your conversation, maintaining eye contact with the person you're talking to, while using your peripheral vision to scan "Mr. Sexy" from head to toe, with nobody the wiser.

So before you judge a man's refrigerator blindness or shocking lack of color sense, just know that you're looking at the world through a different pair of lenses—literally!

Hearing

Research has also shown that women are better than men at distinguishing tone and pitch changes when interacting with others—important skills when tending to the needs of your children and having to determine the difference between the "Mommy, I'm hungry" cry versus the "Mommy, I have a wet diaper" cry, something many men won't catch.[5]

This heightened sensitivity also gives women a distinct advantage in decoding others' feelings by catching the nuances of tone (and meaning) that occur in conversations with other adults. (Women also hold this advantage in the visual realm by reading the micro-expressions playing across a person's face.)

Though emotional intelligence can be increased, most women seem to be born with a giant satellite dish for receiving emotional cues (an important attribute for heading off potential conflict with the other women in the tribe), compared to the basic cable subscription given to most men (since avoiding conflict was less important to his survival). A friend of mine, after years of being in a relationship, once told me, "When communicating with a man, be direct. Men don't speak 'Hint.'"

Smell and Taste

Have you ever wondered why your man (and/or your kids) shove the milk carton in your face and ask, "Is this bad?" Or how you notice the stench of the garbage that needs to be taken out long before he does? It's because you as a woman have more olfactory cells, that's why.

For thousands of years, women in their role as gatherers were in charge of feeding their families and keeping their loved ones safe and healthy. Having a strong sense of smell allowed women to detect noxious odors before they could harm anyone. Combined with a more acute sense of taste—women have more taste buds on their tongues—this quality helped them to identify spoiled or rotten food.[6]

So the next time the man in your life doesn't comment on your new perfume or "ooh and ahh" about the added basil in your new recipe, don't hold it against him. There's a good chance his sniffer, and his tongue, are simply less sensitive.

Touch

A man's skin tends to be thicker and less sensitive than a woman's skin.[7] Anthropologists suggest this may have developed over thousands of years to protect hunters like Grog, who ran through thorny terrain, suffered attacks from larger predators, and were often wounded during regular skirmishes with rival tribes.

Women, on the other hand, have more nerve receptors in their skin and are more sensitive to touch and to pain.[8] That sensitivity increases or decreases with your menstrual cycle.[9] This could be one reason why what feels good to your man might not feel as good to you—and vice versa.

The Golden Rule, "Treat others how you would like to be treated," isn't the best advice for relationships. Instead, upgrade to the "Platinum Rule" and ask your partner what feels good to them, and do more of that.

— Everyday Behaviors —

Now let's explore some of the activities that men and women naturally gravitate toward and the feel-good chemicals those activities stimulate.

Let's start with men. Most masculine men are attracted to activities that stimulate a brain chemical called dopamine, such as competing, fighting, achieving goals, being productive, taking risks, problem-solving, increasing efficiency, and so on.[10]

Notice the parallels between these activities and the activities of Grog, our hunter? It makes sense that Grog would get a biochemical boost when he competed with others, took risks, and achieved goals (for example, caught lunch)—all activities that helped him and his family survive.

As a woman, you also feel great when receiving a hit of dopamine. No one is saying that women don't love to be productive or solve problems. However, it's useful to notice that most feminine women tend to gravitate toward activities that stimulate a different hormone, called oxytocin.[11]

Oxytocin is known as the "bonding chemical" and helps us feel in love and emotionally in synch with one another.[12] For example, some of the activities that trigger oxytocin are gazing in another person's eyes, holding hands, or spending time together.[13] Notice how all these activities are a form of connection? Connection gives the feminine that beautiful hit of oxytocin she's after.

Two other fabulous oxytocin boosters are contribution and collaboration—this is why you're always finding ways to be helpful and make things better for those around you. Activities that involve communication, like having great conversations, also give you an oxytocin charge.[14] And of course, cuddling; even just softly stroking your skin stirs up that sweet feel-good chemical![15]

Notice the parallels between our gatherer Mog's activities and the ones listed above? Mog got a biochemical bonus when she collaborated well with others, contributed to those around her, communicated with her tribe, and cuddled with her babies—all things that helped to ensure her family had the best chance of thriving.

These are just a few examples of the ways masculine and feminine energy perceive and move through the world differently. The more you begin to notice these differences—not just in your partner, but in yourself—the more empowered you become. Because when you understand how your man is wired, you stop taking the disconnects personally.

If he doesn't want to snuggle the same way you do? It might just not be his jam. If he doesn't share every detail of his day? It's not rejection—it's just not how he processes. If you're hoping to sit and connect over a glass of wine, but he's tossing you a Ping-Pong paddle and saying, "Loser does the dishes!" it's not that he doesn't want to be close; it's that his brain is in full-on "need-dopamine" mode. Right now, talking about feelings isn't his game plan.

Understanding his tendencies gives you access to deeper connection, while owning what lights you up invites him to meet you there. So if your guy occasionally disappears into his cave, it's not always a red flag. Sometimes, it's just him being . . . a masculine man. Processing. Resetting. Finding his footing so he can come back stronger.

Your power is in your awareness. In holding your center. In trusting the natural rhythm of masculine and feminine energy—how it contracts and expands, pulls away and returns, like the tide.

Now that you're grounded in the energetic truths of the masculine and feminine, you can harness their incredible power for one of the most exciting parts of this journey: igniting attraction. You're about to step into Part Two, where we shift from insight to ignition. Get ready to learn the key actions that will spark a magnetic fire of desire in your man's heart, mind, and body—whether you're dating, deep in partnership, or somewhere in between.

Let's turn up the heat.

Part Two

Igniting Attraction

Chapter Four

Becoming Irresistible

— There's Just Something About Her —

Connor leaned back in his chair, beer in hand, eyes lit up like he'd just seen a sunrise no one else had noticed.

"I don't know, man . . ." he said to his best friend, shaking his head and letting out a half-laugh, half-sigh. "There's just something about her. She's not like anyone I've ever met."

His buddy raised an eyebrow. "Yeah? How so?"

Connor paused, eyes drifting to some far-off place, like he was trying to capture a feeling too big for words.

"It's just . . . easy with her," he said, shaking his head with a soft laugh. "I don't have to be anything but me. No front. No trying to impress her. It's like she brings out the best parts of me without even trying. And when I'm with her . . . I actually like who I am."

There's just something about her.

She's different.

She makes life feel lighter, connection feel deeper, and being a man feel *better*.

What Connor was experiencing—that magnetic, irresistible pull—wasn't about her looks (though he definitely found her beautiful). It was something deeper and more powerful. It was her energy. Her presence. The way she moved through the world with a feminine aliveness that awakened something inside of him. To him, she had that special "it" factor. An intangible quality he couldn't quite put into words but that was unmistakably present.

Many people believe that some women are born with this kind of allure and others aren't—as if it's some magical trait sprinkled on them at birth. But lucky for all of us, that's not true. That *falling-for-her* experience Connor had? That magnetism? That irresistible energy? It's not magic. It's a learnable, repeatable combination of three powerful ingredients:

- Igniting attraction
- Deepening emotional connection
- Skillfully communicating

The good news is, every woman can attract the type of man that *just gets them* . . . when she understands how the process works.

In this section of the book, we're going to explore the first of the above powerful ingredients: what creates that spark—that magnetic force that makes a man not just notice you, but feel *pulled* toward you. The kind of attraction that makes him lean in, prioritize you, and feel like he's found something rare.

This chapter is your guide to understanding and activating the kind of feminine energy that makes a man feel "There's just something about her . . ." Not because you're trying harder. Not because you're changing who you are. But because you're learning how to amplify the *truth* of who you are in a way that naturally awakens his masculine energy—and ignites a powerful attraction that feels exciting, easy, and real.

To assist you in unleashing even more of your irresistible feminine energy, I gathered more than a hundred of the best techniques from thousands of women in my workshops and coaching communities. Then I narrowed them down to eight of the most powerful, user-friendly practices that amplify your feminine energy and at the same time activate his masculine energy—supercharging the intensity of attraction he feels for you.

Now you may be asking yourself, *What if my man isn't super masculine?* Here's the good news. You'll be amazed at how the space you create by amplifying your own feminine energy naturally draws your man into his masculine energy. This feeds your feminine energy further, which boosts his masculine energy, which makes your feminine energy blossom even more, and on and on, creating a beautiful upward spiral of growing polarity. And as both your energies increase, your attraction to each other will skyrocket!

To help you remember these eight practices more easily, I've created an acronym using the word "feminine."

— F.E.M.I.N.I.N.E. —

As you learn the practices that follow, remember, you don't need to do all eight of them all the time. Sometimes just one of them is enough to help you lean in to your feminine energy and ignite attraction.

F—Feel Your Body

What are you feeling in your body right now? Notice the sensation of the air on your face. Notice the feeling of your clothes touching your skin. Place your attention on your heart-center. Notice the emotions or energy your heart is experiencing in this moment.

For many people, experiencing their body and heart's energy is a rare occurrence. It's so easy to get stuck in our heads and become numb or disconnected from our bodies. Especially if we're working full time, solving problems, leading teams, and accomplishing goals.

One of the fastest ways to shift from masculine energy (head/thinking) into feminine energy (heart/feeling) is to close your eyes and take three long, slow, deep breaths. Then direct your attention to your heart-center. While your attention is on your heart, simply notice your physical body. This easy, yet powerful, move connects you to your feelings, to your body, and to the present moment. In doing so, you engage your feminine energy.

Another potent method for dropping from your head into your body is dancing. Find a place you can be undisturbed, crank up your favorite playlist, and let your body move in any way it wants to. Besides being a surefire way to ramp up your feminine mojo, it's great exercise!

One last embodiment hack: dive fully into any one of your five senses. Find something in your environment to focus on and pretend you've never seen anything like it before. Really look at the colors, shapes, and textures in whatever object you've chosen. (Nature is a great place to start—a flower, a tree, even the sky can bring you into your embodied self.) Run your hands over the fabric of your chair or your sweater (or your own skin), listen closely to the hum of conversation around you, inhale the fragrance of a flower or of baking cookies, savor the taste of your favorite food or drink.

Feeling your body and being present right where you are gives you confidence and makes you comfortable in your own skin, two qualities no man can resist.

E—Experience Pleasure Deeply

There's almost nothing more captivating to a man than a woman who is overcome with pleasure. This practice builds on the practice of "Feel Your Body." The more deeply you allow yourself to experience pleasure throughout your body, the more exciting and attractive it is for your man.

This principle is especially true when it comes to sexual pleasure, but it also extends far beyond physical arousal. Experiencing pleasure deeply means becoming a sponge that absorbs the delights of life. It means giving yourself permission to relish what tickles your senses and ignites your soul.

Unfortunately, many of us have a pattern of resisting pleasure, not allowing ourselves to feel good. Or, because we live in such a go-go-go society, we focus so much on accomplishing our goals that we literally forget to enjoy life along the way.

To practice experiencing pleasure deeply, start by feeling your body and then amp it up: see how richly or intensely you can enjoy the small pleasures of your day. Savor the sweet taste of your favorite fruit, noticing how the juices awaken your taste buds. Soak in the magnificence of a sunset and allow the beauty to fill your heart with palpable joy. Let your favorite song send tingles down your spine. As you turn up the dial on your pleasure meter, you'll automatically turn up the dial on your man's "attraction" meter.

My sister, Jennifer, shared an experience with me that demonstrates how powerful this practice can be:

Years ago, my then-fiancé/now-husband Jorge and I attended a celebrity wedding in Mexico City. The groom, a friend of Jorge's, was one of Mexico's most famous actors, so several of the guests were also actors—talented Latin stars from different countries like Spain, Argentina, and Colombia. They were gorgeous men and women, looking as if they had stepped straight off the pages of a fashion magazine or movie set.

It was a small, intimate wedding, and after the ceremony we all stood around, chatting and sipping champagne, while music played. I was talking to Jorge, when out of the corner of my eye, I noticed five of the hottest actors there all standing in a line and staring, spellbound. I turned to see what they were looking at and saw the groom's sister, dancing by herself in a small open space at the end of the room.

The woman was completely engrossed in the music, moving her body in uninhibited joyful dance, clueless she was being watched. With her eyes half closed and her hair flying around her, she moved her hips to the beat in undulations, spirals, and circles. It was clear that she was thoroughly enjoying herself, enraptured by the moment.

Although she wasn't the most "conventionally beautiful" woman in the room, without a doubt she was the most attractive, because she was directly connected to her pleasure.

That was when I became aware that being magnetic to men had way less to do with a woman's face, hair, makeup, body, perfume, or clothing and more to do with her ENERGY. What these men were drawn to was the way her spirit animated her body with delight and aliveness. It was truly mesmerizing.

When you allow yourself to feel the pleasure of the moment and experience it fully, you amplify your feminine energy, causing your man to be irresistibly drawn to you.

M—Magnify Your Allowing

A few months before I met Irene, I joined a group of friends for a salsa dancing class at a club in Los Angeles called Mama Juana's. Now, while I'd mastered the classic middle-school "arms-locked-sway" move, I knew absolutely *nada* about salsa.

The first thing the instructor said struck me like a lightning bolt. "Every salsa starts with polarity," he explained. "One person steps forward. The other steps back." The masculine energy—whoever is leading—steps forward with intention. The feminine energy—whoever is following—steps back and creates space. Then he looked at the women in the class and said something I'll never forget:

"Ladies, your power in this dance is in your allowing. The more you try to control the steps, the more you'll clash. But if you trust . . . if you *respond* . . . something beautiful happens. You create the space that calls him to lead." To prove his point, he whispered to his partner, and both stepped forward at the same time—*bam*, they bumped into each other.

"See? Two people leading equals collision." Then they both stepped back. The dance fell flat. No momentum. No flow. He turned to us and grinned. "But when you create space—when the feminine takes that first graceful step back—it invites the masculine to move in. And when the masculine steps forward to meet her . . . that's when the dance begins."

Boom.

That wasn't just a salsa lesson; it was a *relationship revelation*. I realized I had been doing the exact opposite in my dating life. I was stepping back first—waiting, hesitating—inviting women to lead. And over and over again, I found myself with women in their masculine energy, while I struggled to step into mine.

That dance class cracked open something in me.

In relationships, just like in salsa, the masculine leads by stepping forward, and the feminine creates the invitation by stepping back—by allowing space for him to step in. But here's the thing . . .

Allowing doesn't mean being passive. It doesn't mean you don't have desires. It doesn't mean you sit around waiting for a man to read your mind or take control of your life. Allowing means that once you've made a clear request or expressed what you desire, you *release the outcome* and create space for him to provide.

Space is everything, because masculine energy *hates* a vacuum. It's wired to *fill it*. That's why when you allow rather than direct, when you trust rather than control, you activate his masculine core—and draw him closer.

This doesn't mean that you can't ever lead. In fact, in a relationship, the balance of masculine and feminine can evolve over time. What works in early dating—where he takes the lead and you lean back—might shift as you both move into deeper commitment. Maybe you decide to alternate who plans your date nights. Maybe you're the one who maps out the vacation while he handles the logistics. That's awesome—as long as you're co-creating the dynamic together.

What matters most is not who plays which role—but that there's *polarity*, and that you're *consciously creating* your rhythm, your dance, as a couple.

If you're thinking, "But I love planning dates!" or "Sometimes I enjoy being in the lead"—yes! You absolutely can. Just notice what energy you're bringing to it. If it's from love, joy, and choice, it's powerful. But if it's from frustration, control, or fear he won't step up—it won't create the result you want.

To magnify your allowing, try releasing the outcome and empower your man to fill the space by bringing your desire to life. Let him feel that you trust him—and you'll often be amazed at how he rises to the occasion. Just be mindful not to initially let him lead and then take control right in the middle of the dance—that sends a mixed signal: "I want you to lead, but I don't trust you to do it." Instead, allow him to lead in the way he knows how. Even if it's a little different than how *you* would do it.

Because when he feels your trust—your space, your soft allowing—his masculine energy *ignites*. And that ignition is the very fuel that propels attraction.

You may find this practice especially challenging if you're dating and the relationship isn't progressing as quickly as you'd like. The masculine energy in you wants to grab the reins: *He's too slow—just ask him out.*

Or maybe you're already in a relationship, and your partner hasn't planned anything romantic in a while. You might feel tempted to do it all yourself just to keep the spark alive. But hang tight. Because in the next section, you're going to learn how to *initiate feminine invitations*—the kind that light a fire under his masculine energy, without ever having to chase or push. And this is where things really start to sizzle.

I—Initiate Invitations

One of the misconceptions about feminine energy is that it's passive or inactive, or it must always "follow" while masculine energy always "leads."

This couldn't be further from the truth. Feminine energy is highly proactive and can initiate in any situation. The difference is in *how* you're proactive and *how* you lead. Your feminine energy pulls a man toward you—in contrast to your masculine energy, which pursues.

To be proactive and feminine, all you need to do is simply invite him to provide you with something you want. If you want him to come talk to you, you could send him an interested look combined with a subtle smile. Or if your style is more outgoing, you could even wave him over to you. In either case, this body language acts as the "first step back" that creates an energetic space, pulling him toward you. He reads this signal as the request, "Will you provide me with what I want?" This inspires his masculine energy to fill the space you've created.

If you're in a relationship, you can initiate invitations by asking him to create an experience you would enjoy or to help you in some way. The difference between masculine and feminine leading is small but powerful. Masculine energy leads in this way: "Want to go hiking this weekend? I've got a great hike picked out." Feminine energy leads by initiating an invitation (or making a request): "I'd love to go hiking this weekend. Would you plan it for us?"

Masculine energy says: "Let's go to our favorite breakfast place." Feminine energy says: "I'm really craving our favorite breakfast place. Would you plan a time for us to go?" Masculine energy says: "Let's grab a drink after work." Feminine energy says: "I could really use some time to unwind. Would you take me out for a drink after work?"

Notice how the masculine pursues (or plans) and the feminine pulls (or requests), creating a space for the masculine to provide what the feminine wants.

Here's an easy feminine formula for initiating invitations. You can simply say, "I would love [insert what you want]. Will you [plan it, create it, make it happen, take me]?" This format of initiating invitations is incredibly effective at igniting his masculine energy. Don't be surprised if you see your man leap into action when you make these kinds of requests.

Like many of my clients, at first you may feel resistant to using these phrases because you're afraid that it makes you sound needy or dependent on a man to do something. But if you're willing to try them out, I think you'll find the opposite is true—you'll feel incredibly empowered because you're directly asking for what you want and allowing it to come to you.

Now again, you don't have to live in your feminine energy all the time. In a relationship, the two of you will most likely share the planning of your activities or date nights. Initiating invitations is a great tool to use anytime you want to consciously amplify your feminine energy and draw your man into his masculine.

You can see how these practices work in concert with one another. When you initiate invitations, magnify your allowing, and enjoy receiving, it creates an irresistible combination that stokes his attraction.

N—Nourish Your Needs

It's tough to be at your best when your needs aren't being met. If you're stressed, overwhelmed, hungry, or tired, your feminine radiance doesn't stand a chance.

Over the years, I've spoken with thousands of women who've shared with me that the challenge in taking care of themselves is that they're instinctively wired to put the needs of everyone else ahead of their own, including the needs of their man and/or children. Women say they feel guilty at the thought of nourishing their needs first—especially if someone they care about needs something at that same moment.

If you've ever felt that way, give yourself permission to cast that guilt aside and prioritize nourishing your needs. If your needs go unmet long enough, you'll burn yourself out, and when that happens, it's too easy to snap at the people who mean the most to you, sabotaging the acts of love you were trying to give them in the first place.

So whether it's grabbing food, exercising, taking a nap, soaking in a bath, getting a manicure, or simply going for a walk (some of the go-to activities my clients and communities have shared), giving yourself what you need is essential for being at your best and relaxing into your feminine energy.

What most women don't realize is that if you ask a man if he'd prefer you get a task done in that moment or delay the task so you can take care of your needs and get back to it later, a high-quality man will support you in taking care of your needs.

For an added bonus, enlist your man in helping you meet your needs. An easy way to do this is to frame your request as a favor and let him know the impact it would have on you: "Would you be willing to run a bath for me? It would make a huge difference in my day." That way you accomplish two things at once: your needs get met *and* he gets to provide what you want (fueling his masculine energy). It's a win all around. So go ahead; ask for what you need in the moment. Because what your man needs is for his woman to feel good.

I—Inhabit Your Softness

Another great way to amplify your feminine energy is to reveal your gentle or soft side to your man. This can be as simple as using a gentle tone of voice or offering a feathery touch—such as gently stroking his jawline with the soft pads of your fingertips.

You can also demonstrate your soft side by "melting into your man." A masculine man absolutely loves to feel his partner completely relax into his body. Here are some examples that women in my programs have shared: when you hug him, relax, and let your body and energy rest in his arms. When you're snuggling in bed, lay your head on your man's chest with your leg draped over his body, completely let go, and allow your full energy to melt into his. Whatever helps you activate your soft, gentle nature will, in turn, draw him into his masculine energy, leading to a stronger attraction between you.

Ellen, a client of mine who described herself as driven, passionate about her career, and competitive, once asked me, "I have challenges being soft. Will that push men away?" My answer to her question was, "Not if you know how to shift in and out of feminine energy when you want." It can actually be an advantage to have both energies! Expressing more masculine energy at times presents a beautiful opportunity to create even more attraction. Here's why: instead of being "monotone" and only coming from your feminine energy all the time, the woman who is dynamic enough to demonstrate both energies in different moments in her life makes the relationship exciting.

When your man sees you shift from your "ass-kicking, goal-achieving" masculine drive into your feminine softness by melting into him, you send an unmistakable message that you feel safe enough with him to relax into your feminine energy. This creates an enormous charge of masculine energy in him and boosts the attraction.

Regardless of where you are on the masculine–feminine spectrum, inhabiting your softness is a beautiful technique for activating the polarity of feminine and masculine energies.

N—Nurture Connection

To amplify your feminine energy, make it a priority to connect with your girlfriends or the other important relationships in your life. Create time to get together with the people you enjoy being around. Pour energy into each other. Talk, laugh, and connect—all activities that stimulate your feminine feel-good chemical, oxytocin.

Remember Mog? Every day, she worked with the other women in her tribe—her friends, sisters, aunts, mom, and grandmothers—chatting, connecting, and contributing to one another.

Life today is different, and it's often challenging to make good female friends, especially as an adult! If that's the case, don't give up. Many women find connection through joining women's groups based on an enjoyable activity—for example, meet-up groups, hiking groups, cooking groups, book clubs, or volunteer groups.

As you deepen these new connections, you'll find that this time away will fill your emotional cup. When you get home, you'll be radiant, full of joy, and feel sky-high. Your man will take one look at you and say, "Wow, you should go out with your girlfriends more often."

E—Embrace Your Sexy-Self

The final strategy shared by the women in my community for activating feminine energy is to own your sexiness, or, in other words, see yourself as the sexy woman you are.

So many women described how easy it is to self-criticize, to focus on the parts of their body that feel unattractive—especially those areas that protrude or sag or aren't as smooth and firm as they used to be. But they also reported that when they adopted the mindset that their sexiness isn't determined by how "perfect" their body is but rather an energy or attitude they embody, they activated a profound shift in how sexy they felt, and their partners responded in kind.

Here's a concept that can support you in embracing that sexy-self mindset: connect to the way that your ideal man sees you. I would argue that that man sees you as *way* sexier than that nasty little critical voice wants you to believe. Most men are not nitpicking those areas that aren't "perfect." Instead, what they see is the beautiful gestalt of the feminine body. When you own your sexiness and feel that you're desirable, it's like pouring gasoline on the fire of attraction—your man's desire for you will rise a few hundred degrees.

To help physically activate sexy energy, some women said wearing lingerie or silky clothing puts them in their sensual mode. For others, dancing, either with a partner or alone, to just the right music brings them to a heated boil. Many women find their sexy-self by reading or watching love scenes in their favorite books or films.

But most women said that their biggest shifts in this area came from changing their attitude about themselves and recognizing that embracing their sexiness was a choice they could make whenever they wanted, regardless of how "imperfect" their body was. This powerful new mindset gave them the liberation to flirt more, be more playful, and radiate their sexual energy.

Of course, there will be times you're exhausted from the day, or just not in the mood, and that's called being human. Those are the moments to focus on yourself and to nourish your needs. You'll find that the more your cup is filled up, the easier it is to connect with your sexual energy. Most men are aware of this dynamic and will support you in giving yourself what you need. Smart men know if they do, it won't be long until the two of you are "getting your snuggle on!"

Let's recap the eight F.E.M.I.N.I.N.E. energy practices for becoming irresistible:

F – Feel Your Body
E – Experience Pleasure Deeply
M – Magnify Your Allowing
I – Initiate Invitations
N – Nourish Your Needs
I – Inhabit Your Softness
N – Nurture Connection
E – Embrace Your Sexy-Self

You might find that you're very good at some of these practices, and more challenged by others. It's worth the effort to get comfortable with as many as you can, so that you have a variety of tools in your toolbox to create the attraction you want in any situation. Simply knowing how to dial up your feminine energy gives you the opportunity to increase polarity in your relationship and naturally ignite attraction whenever you want.

Take my coaching client Sharon for example.

Sharon was a powerhouse—a top criminal defense attorney known for her tenacity in the courtroom. From the outside, she seemed to have it all together, but underneath, she was exhausted, lonely, and frustrated. For years, she'd been living with an emotionally checked-out husband, essentially acting as a single mom even while married.

After she and her husband divorced, Sharon began dating, determined to find a great guy. But every time she swiped right, it was the same story: emotionally unavailable men, hot and cold behavior, and lots of first dates that never went anywhere.

The deeper truth? Sharon was replaying an old, painful script—one that said she wasn't enough. Growing up, her parents had been extremely strict and only praised her when she brought home straight As or won awards. Subconsciously, she'd absorbed the belief that love was something you had to earn.

So, she overcompensated. She led with her résumé, her accomplishments, her checklist of "look how great I am" rather than the radiant, feminine woman underneath. She was so busy proving she was "enough" that she never slowed down to receive the love she craved.

After years of hit-and-miss dating, mostly misses, she decided to join my Manifest Your Man program. Over the next few months, Sharon dove deep into learning the feminine superpowers. She started by owning her value and focusing on being fully present. She practiced being in her body and nourishing her own needs—taking long walks, soaking in bubble baths, and journaling about how she wanted to feel in a relationship. By filling herself up, she stopped trying to impress men and started being fully present with them. Sharon also learned to embrace her softness. She had always been in "battle mode"—ready to debate, ready to lead. Now, she practiced softening her tone, leaning back, and allowing men to contribute.

When Mark—a man she met online who was warm and generous—asked her out to dinner, she didn't jump to suggest the restaurant or insist on splitting the bill. Instead, she said, "I'd love to go somewhere with great ambiance. Would you choose a place and take me?" To her surprise, Mark was thrilled. He picked her up, opened her door, and planned the entire evening. Sharon was delighted at how the experience was so easy and just seemed to flow.

One evening, after a particularly sweet date with Mark, she felt that old urge to overcompensate. *How can I make sure he doesn't feel like I'm taking advantage of him?* When she next saw Mark, she asked, "What can I give you? How can I contribute?"

He smiled and said simply, "Just appreciate me. That's the best gift you can give me." So she did, acknowledging Mark for all the big and small ways he showed up for her. For the first time, Sharon felt the power of allowing herself to be seen and cherished, without earning it, without proving anything, just by being herself.

A few months later, Sharon read an article about the holiday festivities in Solvang, a charming town up the coast. The old Sharon would have just booked the outing herself. But now, she said to Mark, "Oh, I've heard that Solvang is beautiful at Christmas. It would be so wonderful to go there! Would you be willing to take me?" He took the lead, planning the entire day, and the two of them had a magical weekend that Sharon didn't have to orchestrate or manage. It was the beginning of a whole new chapter in her life—one where she didn't have to carry the mental load of the relationship. One where she got to receive and be cherished by a man who loved her for exactly who she was.

GIFT BOX

Want a powerful meditation to amplify your feminine energy? Click here to download "The Femininity Meditation."

Chapter Five

His Deepest Desire

The argument started over dishes.

It always starts small. Two plates, a coffee mug, and a half-eaten sandwich crust sat in the sink—just inches from the garbage can and empty dishwasher below. That's all it took to set off the latest spiral.

"Seriously, Mike?" Katie's voice rang out from the kitchen doorway. "You couldn't take two seconds to put the dishes in the dishwasher?"

Mike looked up from his laptop, blinking. "I was going to load them when I got up."

"Right. Just like you were 'going to' send those client emails yesterday. Or 'going to' follow up with that lead from last week." Her tone had an edge to it. Not yelling. Just sharp. Clipped. Exhausted.

He said nothing. Just closed his laptop.

Katie turned and walked back into the kitchen, her shoulders stiff, her jaw tight. She wasn't trying to be cruel. In her mind, she was just being honest. She was tired of feeling like she was the only adult in the house, tired of carrying the load—financially, emotionally, even keeping the house together. They hadn't had sex in over six months. Conversations had dwindled to logistics: What time is the dentist appointment? Can you pick up milk? Did you pay the water bill?

The connection they once had—the flirtation, the laughter, the sense of being on the same team—felt like a different lifetime. Mike stayed on the couch, rubbing the back of his neck. He hated fighting. But more than that, he hated this version of himself: the man who couldn't seem to get his footing, the man whose wife now looked at him with irritation instead of admiration.

When he lost his corporate job almost a year ago, he thought it would be a turning point. A chance to finally build his dream business. Do something meaningful. Make his own hours, be his own boss. But it turned out starting a business was harder than he thought. Progress was slow. He'd hit wall after wall—and every time he hesitated, Katie seemed to tighten the screws a little more.

What she called "motivating him" felt like judgment. Like she didn't believe in him. Like he was a disappointment.

What he hadn't told her—what he couldn't find the words for—was how crushed he felt. How small. How ashamed. He didn't want to defend himself. He just wanted to disappear. Later that night, they lay on opposite ends of the bed in silence. Katie scrolled on her phone. Mike stared at the ceiling. She turned out the light without saying good night. He rolled over and faced the wall. Neither of them knew how to fix it. Neither of them knew how to say what they really needed. But one thing was clear: The distance between them had never felt greater.

Most people assume that what a man wants most is sex. And while physical intimacy is certainly important to him, it's not actually the deepest driver of his heart. Beneath the surface lies a longing that runs far deeper: A man wants to feel respected.

For a masculine man, respect is more than just appreciation—it's the oxygen his soul breathes. It tells him he's valued, trusted, and seen as capable. And when that respect begins to erode—especially from the woman he loves—it cuts to the core of his identity. You can tell a man "I love you" a hundred times, but if he feels like you don't respect him, those words won't land. They won't feel real.

Over time, the absence of respect will shut a man down emotionally, mentally, and even physically. If he doesn't feel like he measures up in your eyes, it becomes nearly impossible for him to open up, to lead, to engage . . . and yes, even to perform sexually. Respect, to him, isn't optional. It's essential.

IMPORTANT NOTE: All the material in this section is based on the assumption that you're with a man worthy of your respect—someone honorable, who strives to keep his agreements, and respects you in return. Of course, there are bad guys out there you'd do well to avoid, but our focus is on those men who aim to do the right thing, and who are also human and imperfect.

So, what does respecting your man really mean? Does it mean never disagreeing? Never challenging his ideas? Not having an opposing opinion? Of course not. A lot of people in high-functioning relationships enjoy having healthy debates with one another. It's entirely possible for couples to challenge or disagree with each other *in a respectful way*, which means valuing and treating the other person with dignity, even if you don't agree.

For a man, one of the purest forms of respect is appreciation. Your authentic acknowledgment of his effectiveness providing the experience you want is inextricably tied to his self-worth. Remember Grog, our hunter? When he came through the cave opening, dragging dinner behind him, Mog's response in that moment had a huge impact on how Grog felt about himself and the job he'd just done. If she was thrilled, celebrating his vital accomplishment, he experienced a wave of positive emotion—success, joy, fulfillment. If she was unimpressed or ungrateful, then he not only felt his efforts didn't meet the mark, but he also felt inadequate as a man.

You have more power than you realize to influence how your man feels. Your man's sense of worth has less to do with what he's providing, and much more to do with how what he's providing impacts you. I'm not advising feigning a positive response or blowing sunshine at him when he hasn't earned it. What I am saying, however, is that when you genuinely acknowledge or appreciate his job well done, you hit the bullseye of your man's deepest desire: to be respected. This produces an especially pleasurable feeling inside of him—a spark that ignites the fire of attraction, if you will.

If you want to turn that spark into a dazzling blaze, there are two specific behaviors you can embrace that unmistakably demonstrate your respect for a man. I call them the Two Cs:

1. Count on His Competence
2. Celebrate His Job Well Done

These two expressions of respect are food for his soul and will radically draw him closer to you. The Two Cs contain the two most potent elements of respect: trust and appreciation. Used separately, they're highly effective, but when you make a habit of using them both, it's a magical combination that men find incredibly hard to resist!

— Count on His Competence —

One of the best forms of respecting a man is to show him you have confidence in his ability to provide what you want in the relationship. Whether that's taking you out on a great date, cooking a meal for you, or helping you with a project, demonstrating confidence in him looks like requesting that he do something for you, then stepping back and trusting him to get the job done.

There are two common behaviors that cripple trust and push him away—I call them the attraction-killers:

Unsolicited advice: telling your man a better way to accomplish a task when he hasn't asked for help

Micromanaging: inspecting every step he takes to ensure he's doing a task the right way

If you're not aware of these attraction-killing traps, they're easy to fall into. Why? Because they are both expressions of the feminine's instinctual desire to contribute. The feminine loves to help those around them. When a feminine woman knows a better way to accomplish the task, she often offers unsolicited advice. She believes this "contribution" is helpful and will create closeness—which in many cases it does, but in a romantic context, her masculine man will frequently experience her advice as evidence that she doesn't trust him, so it often has the opposite effect, pushing him away. Whenever a woman micromanages a man, especially after having asked for his help, it tells him that she doesn't believe he can do the job for her.

Both these attraction-killing behaviors can trigger his *I'm not enough* fear. Because in his mind, if you believed he was enough, you would have confidence in his ability to accomplish the task. This might sound ridiculous or hypersensitive on his part. I get it. Taking your well-meant advice and direction as lack of trust is clearly a misunderstanding. But don't dismiss the reality or importance of these two nasty little attraction-killers. These "misunderstandings" have contributed to countless arguments and breakups, as well as far too many relationships never getting their fair start.

One of my clients, Lauren, had an epiphany after learning this concept. Lauren is an Ivy League professor and incredibly intelligent, with a natural love for teaching and helping those around her. Despite these sterling qualities, Lauren wasn't having much luck attracting the kind of man she wanted in her life. She had lots of "first and fizzle" dates—first dates that started out strong but quickly fizzled out. For some reason the attraction and connection just weren't there.

After learning that men perceive unsolicited advice and micromanagement as not being trusted, Lauren recognized an unconscious pattern at work in her love life. She thought back to her last date with a guy named Tom. He asked to take Lauren out to the movies, and she happily agreed. Driving on the freeway to the movie theatre, Lauren spotted their exit approaching and promptly told Tom to move into the right lane because the exit was coming up. After all, she didn't want them to miss the exit.

Then driving through the parking lot, Lauren noticed a spot open up in front of the movie theatre. She told Tom to head down the next aisle and take the open parking spot. While Tom was being polite and following Lauren's suggestions, she remembered noticing a small shift in his energy. Even though she was simply being helpful, she now saw how his masculine energy translated "helpfulness" into "She's not confident in me."

Although Lauren was trying to score points by being helpful, she ended up losing points with Tom. Her small contributions didn't let him prove that he had what it took to provide the experience she wanted. He interpreted her instructions as evidence that she didn't trust him to not miss the exit or find a reasonable parking spot. Here's the kicker: Because he didn't feel trusted, he didn't get the feeling of validation for creating the experience she desired. Without this emotional reward, the attraction (and the connection) suffered.

One of the best ways to show your man trust is to let him lead. When you sit back, relax, and let him take charge, you demonstrate through your actions that you have confidence in his ability to deliver the result you want. This might be easier said than done, especially if you've had experiences of being let down by important men in your life: for example, your dad left your family, your husband betrayed you, or your former partners rarely followed through. In that case, trusting can be really challenging, and even scary. The problem is, if you have a pattern of not trusting men, you may be pushing honorable, masculine men away. Honorable men need to feel your trust in a relationship.

If you've been let down in the past, here's a simple way you can begin building trust, at any point in the relationship: give your man small opportunities to keep his word. For example, when you accept an invitation to go out with him and he shows up at the agreed hour, or calls at the time he says he's going to call, or plans the date and then communicates that plan in advance.

When he follows through, make a mental note of the trust credit he just deposited into your relationship bank account. Over time, as he continues to deposit trust credits, you'll have the history and the confidence to give him more of your trust going forward.

Remember, a man's sense of worth is connected to what he's providing for you. Even a small task, like taking you to the movies, has a beautiful payoff for a man when the woman he likes simply receives his "gift." Your acts of trust are small sparks that ignite a very big fire of attraction.

Lauren's insight inspired her to try an experiment. Over the course of the next few months, when dating, Lauren decided not to offer little helpful bits of advice and instead sit back and let her date lead. This adjustment paid major dividends, especially because she combined it with celebrating his job well done.

— Celebrate His Job Well Done —

After learning about masculine and feminine energy, Lauren made a conscious decision to shift how she was showing up on her dates. Instead of trying to control the experience or offer "helpful suggestions," she began experimenting with relaxing into her feminine energy—receiving, appreciating, and simply allowing. That shift led to two major breakthroughs.

The first came when she noticed how much easier it was becoming to let go of control. Even though it still took a little effort not to steer the date, she found herself able to breathe more deeply, lean back, and trust the process. She could feel her receptivity growing—and with it, her enjoyment of the moment.

The second breakthrough came when she witnessed how the men she was dating responded to simple acknowledgment. On one date, when her date picked a fantastic little bistro tucked away on a quiet street, she smiled and said, "Wow, I love this place. Great choice!" She watched as his shoulders straightened and a quiet grin spread across his face. It was subtle, but powerful. Just that one moment of appreciation made him light up. Lauren was amazed. It felt effortless, even fun—and yet the impact was undeniable. The more she relaxed into her feminine energy and celebrated what was working, the more drawn her dates were to her.

And then she met Andrew. From the very first date, she could feel something different. Andrew had a grounded presence that made it easy for her to relax. Instead of defaulting to suggestions or critiques, she leaned back, received what he offered, and celebrated his efforts. Whether it was choosing a restaurant or planning their next outing, she simply acknowledged him: "This is amazing. Thank you for putting thought into this." And Andrew? He soaked it in.

That first date turned into a second, then a third, and soon they were seeing each other regularly. Over time, their connection deepened into something truly special—a passionate, supportive, soul-nourishing relationship. Lauren realized that all the practice she'd done—the shifts in her energy, her willingness to try a new approach, and her courage to trust the process—had paid off in the most beautiful way.

When you celebrate your man for a job well done by praising him with your words or actions, you show him that he's enough for you. In those moments, your man will feel deeply respected for his efforts and have a profound appreciation for you.

Of course, great relationships require both people to show up fully. Your man's job is to praise and acknowledge you as well, to cherish you and love you the way you want to be loved. When you're willing to reach out with respect, it has incredible power to inspire your man to give you what you want in return. As you both practice giving to each other in ways that satisfy your deeper desires, the love you both experience expands.

If you're looking for some simple yet highly effective words you can say that will show your man that you appreciate his effort and respect his thinking, here are some surefire phrases to ignite his deepest desire:

Good decision . . .

"Good decision to call ahead and get reservations; this place is packed."

Perfect choice . . .

"Perfect choice! This gift is wonderful."

Great idea . . .

"This hike was a great idea! Thank you for planning this."

Brilliant . . .

"That's a brilliant idea. Let's do it!"

I appreciate you . . .

"Thank you for driving to my side of town; I appreciate you so much."

NOTE: Notice the difference between "I appreciate it" versus "I appreciate you." When you use the word "it," you place the focus of your gratitude on the thing he's done, in this case the driving time he saved you. But when you replace the word "it" with "you," you focus your gratitude on him—and he feels the reward of your acknowledgment even more strongly.

Here are some more examples:

"You saved the day!"

I discovered the power of this phrase by chance. On a vacation one year, my wife and kids waited in the car while I ran into the grocery store for a few items. When I returned with ice cream bars, my five-year-old daughter said, "Yay, Dad! You saved the day!" Her words made me laugh but also gave me an unexpected burst of positive feeling. I was surprised at the strong emotional effect her words had on me. Whether your man really does save the day, or you use this phrase in a playful way when he does something small but nice for you—like running an errand—either way you'll get a great response from him.

"Thank you for having my back."

This phrase is pure gold because it lets your man know that you notice his efforts to support you and that you deeply appreciate them. Whether he's defending you in a conversation, taking on a task you needed help with, or simply being there to listen when you're feeling overwhelmed, acknowledging his protective and supportive side will make him feel like your hero. Saying "Thank you for having my back when I needed it" reassures him that his efforts to protect and provide for you aren't going unnoticed.

"I love the way you handled that."

This phrase works like a charm because it's both specific and affirming. Whether he navigated a tricky conversation, solved a problem, or made a great decision, pointing it out helps him feel competent and effective. You could say, "I love the way you handled that phone call with the contractor—you were so calm and assertive." Not only does this acknowledge his strength, but it also reinforces that you're paying attention to the way he shows up for you and for others.

"You do a great job of being my man."

This one is guaranteed to knock his socks off! I call it the U.P.P.—the Ultimate Praise Phrase! One evening, my wife and I were driving to a party, and after a few minutes of silence she looked over at me and said, "You know something, babe? You do a great job of being my man."

Boom! Her words hit the bull's-eye, validating my deepest desire to be enough for her. And then she put the cherry on top by listing several specific things she sincerely appreciated about me. Naturally, when I got to the party I was walking on air.

Again, this isn't about false appreciation or feeding your man's ego. It's about being on the lookout for things he's doing right and sincerely acknowledging his actions. Likewise, he should acknowledge you and give you love in the ways that matter most to you. If you want to receive more love in your relationship, start by giving more love to your man. When you focus on giving, you'll be astonished at how he naturally gives back to you.

Relationships are best when both partners are generous with their praise and appreciation. A person who feels filled up fills up others.

— How and When to Offer Advice —

If you want to give your man guidance on a task in a way that feels more supportive and loving to him than offering unsolicited advice, here's an elegant move you can make: *Ask him an empowered question.* Here are some examples of empowered questions:

- "I have a technique that's really helped me in situations like this. Would you like me to share it, or do you feel like you've got it covered?"
- "I have a perspective that's made a big difference for me in similar situations. Would you like to hear it, or are you good with how things are going?"
- "I'm here if you need an extra hand. Would you like me to jump in, or do you want to tackle it solo?"
- "How best can I support you right now?"

Notice that all these questions allow him to gracefully accept or decline your offer to help. There are times when your man is going to love receiving your support, and there are other times when he really wants to accomplish the task on his own. Leading with empowered questions works like magic to maintain the attraction and connection with your man.

When you offer him empowered questions like these, you show him that you believe in his abilities and you're in his corner if he wants help. The key here is that he feels empowered to choose to receive the help or not.

In contrast, jumping in and saying, "Let me show you a better way to do that." Or "You're doing that wrong; try it like this." Or asking disempowering questions like, "Are you sure you know what you're doing?" shows him that you don't believe in his abilities. Remember, a man's greatest desire is to feel respected. Showing him that you believe he is capable of doing "the job" (even if it takes him longer or if he makes a mistake) is one of the best ways to ignite his feeling of being respected.

Many women in my courses ask, *When should I offer advice, and when should I just step back and let it go?* The following rule of thumb may be helpful: If you ask him to lead, then let him lead. Here's a more expanded version of that rule: If you ask your man to help you with something or create an experience for you—and he's not going to hurt himself or anyone else in the process—then let him lead.

Here's an over-the-top example of my wife letting me lead that profoundly impacted me a few years ago. I was driving with Irene and the kids to her parents' house for a family barbecue. On the way, I was focused on telling my wife a story that happened earlier that week. When I finished the story, I realized I had missed the exit I usually take. "Oh no," I said, "we missed the exit!"

"I know," Irene replied. "I saw you go by it about half a mile ago."

"What?! Why didn't you say something?" I asked.

"I just assumed you wanted to take the second exit." Either of the two exits lead to Irene's parents' house, but the first one gets you there faster.

I took the next off-ramp and we arrived at her parents' house about five minutes later than if I had taken the first exit.

As we got the kids out of the car, I experienced two sharply contrasting emotions. First, I felt frustrated with myself for missing the first exit. But even stronger than the frustration, I felt a wave of love welling up in my chest for my wife. Frustration, I could understand. But more love? What was that about?

I tuned in to what was going on inside me and examined the underlying thought fueling this intense feeling of love. I realized that my wife so believed in me that even when I didn't take the exit that I usually do she still gave me the benefit of the doubt—she trusted that I had a good reason for my actions. I was astounded that her small expression of trust had created such a powerful feeling. I went into the house. Seeing her working at the sink, I wrapped my arms around her from behind and whispered in her ear, "You're such an amazing partner."

She turned around and smiled, sliding her arms around my neck. "What makes you say that?" I explained my realization of how much her trust meant to me. She kissed me and said, "I do trust you. And next time, would you like my help if I see you're going to miss the exit?"

"Yes," I said, kissing her back. "I'd love that."

Now that you understand a man's deepest desire (respect), you're equipped to learn about his greatest fear.

Chapter Six

His Greatest Fear

The tension had been building all day.

When she said, "Maybe I should just call my dad," it finally boiled over.

Mark froze, halfway under the sink, hands wet, tools scattered around him. The only sound was the slow drip of water hitting the bucket beneath the pipes. Jenna stood behind him, arms crossed, eyeing the growing puddle on the tile floor.

"I mean, he's great with this stuff. He could have it fixed in no time."

Mark pushed himself out from under the sink and sat back on his heels, wiping his hands on a damp towel.

"So now I need your dad to bail me out?"

"That's not what I said."

"No? That's exactly what it sounds like."

Jenna huffed. "I'm just trying to help. You've been under there for hours and it's still leaking. It's not a crime to ask for help."

"You think I don't know what I'm doing? That I'm just wasting time?" Mark shot back.

Jenna sighed. "That's not what I said."

"No, but it's what you meant." His voice was sharp now, rising with each word. "You always do this. Every time I try to handle something, you question me."

"That's not fair," she shot back. "I'm just tired of watching things fall through the cracks. I feel like I have to pick up the slack all the time!"

Mark stood up fast, stepping over the tools. "I'm doing the best I can, Jenna! Sorry I'm not perfect. Sorry I'm not your fantasy handyman or some guy with a magic wrench who never screws anything up."

She opened her mouth, but the look in his eyes stopped her. They stood in silence for a moment, the weight of what wasn't being said pressing into the space between them. Mark wasn't just reacting to a leaky pipe or a few critical words. He was defending something deeper, the question gnawing at the core of almost every man:

Am I enough?

And in that moment, his answer was: *Maybe not.*

— What's Fear Got to Do with It? —

As humans, every one of us has a primary need to feel that we're enough—that we measure up, that we're capable. So many of the fears that prevent us from going after the relationship we want, or any of the big dreams we have, come from the same deeply rooted fear: "I'm not enough."

I often ask my clients, "Which fears get in the way of you attracting your man?" See if any of their answers sound familiar:

- I'm afraid I'm not attractive enough.
- I'm afraid I'm not fun enough.
- I'm afraid I'm not sexy enough.
- I'm afraid I'm not smart enough.
- I'm afraid I'm not interesting enough.
- I'm afraid I'm not confident enough.

Notice how all these fears are variations of that same underlying mega-fear, "I'm not enough."

And it's not just women. Men will often confide similar fears about attracting a relationship to their closest friends:

- I'm not tall enough.
- I don't make enough money.
- I'm not attractive enough.
- I'm not emotionally open enough.
- I'm not interesting enough.
- I can't provide enough of what she wants.

Though everyone has different life experiences, why do we all seem to share this same deep-rooted fear of not being enough and worry about what will happen to us as a result? Perhaps the best answer lies in our survival instincts—another gift from Mog and Grog! All humans come hardwired with this one predominant primal fear.

For hunters, this fear might have sounded like this: What if I'm not fast enough to outrun the predator? What if I'm not a good enough hunter to bring my family sufficient food? What if I'm not strong enough to fight my rivals and win?

For gatherers: What if I'm not skilled enough to find food to help feed us? What if I'm not likable enough to be accepted by the other women of the tribe? What if I'm not attentive enough to see the poisonous snake moving in the grass?

If any one of these fears proved true, the outcome was often fatal. Today, even though the immediate threats to our physical survival are no longer pressing, we still have those factory-installed fears. That's why, when we're dating or in a relationship with someone and our partner says or does something that triggers our "I'm not enough" fear, even though our conscious mind knows we won't die, our subconscious mind doesn't. A wave of heat and fear travels through our entire body because our subconscious mind has just set off our fight, flight, or freeze survival mechanism.

For the masculine man, his greatest fear is a very distinct type of inadequacy. Specifically, inadequacy in his ability to provide you with what you want or protect you in a way that makes you feel safe. It's no exaggeration to say that a man is deathly afraid of not being enough for you.

Think back to his role as the hunter. The hunter's job was to provide for and protect those he loved. The act of providing and protecting activated his masculine energy. Today, when a man fears he's not enough—that he can't provide for or protect you well enough—that fear threatens his very identity.

For a man to feel lasting attraction in the relationship he must feel confident in his competence. A masculine man needs to feel he is capable of delivering the kind of experience that will make you happy.

Ever had a man get irritated or shut down when you gave him instructions on how to do something better? Ever had a man get defensive when he screwed up and you pointed it out? Ever had your man make a huge effort, going out of his way to bring you something you casually mentioned you wanted? Ever had a man spend a long time telling you all the "cool" or "important" things he's up to and you thought, *Why is he bragging like that?*

Most women have had at least one—if not all—of these experiences with a man. What's going on here? These different behaviors all have one common root: the masculine man's deep need to "be enough" for you. This can look like going "above and beyond" to provide you with something you want or recounting all his accomplishments (which can sound an awful lot like bragging). In both cases, your man is simply trying to impress you and measure up to what he thinks you want.

In the case of his negative reactions—which may seem baffling or overblown to you—here's what is happening under the surface for him: If a man lets an event trigger his *I'm inadequate* fear, then he interprets his mistake and any subsequent correction or constructive criticism to mean that he's not doing a good job providing what you want. (That's when his negative mental fear-train really picks up speed.) He'll think,

If I can't provide what she wants, then I must not be enough for her. And if I'm not enough for her, then she'll leave me. And the thought of losing you terrifies him!

For most men, the last part of this mental sequence—the thought that *If I'm not enough for her, then I'll lose her*—usually never reaches his conscious mind. Instead, he simply feels a charge of fear rise in his body, and he responds with fight-or-flight tactics such as defensiveness, countercriticism, or anger, or he simply just shuts down and pulls away.

The point is, he won't be at his best when he's stuck in a state of fear. So while most women interpret their man's defensiveness as "he doesn't care about my feelings or what I want" and get upset, when you're aware of your man's tender place, and you see him get triggered, you can see right through his surface-level defensiveness and interpret it for what it really is: his way of saying, "I'm defending that I'm enough for you."

Having this "emotional X-ray vision" is like unlocking a relationship superpower. It empowers you to stay centered and grounded, even when he gets rattled, because you're not just reacting to his surface behavior anymore. You're tuned in to the *real* story playing out underneath. And when you can respond to the fear behind the defensiveness, instead of getting pulled into the drama of it, you become a powerful catalyst for connection. Together, you can shift the energy and steer the relationship back toward closeness, understanding, and connection.

Sarah, a graduate of my Cracking the Man Code course, told me a story that perfectly illustrates this very point.

Sarah

Not long ago, my husband, Joe, and I came home after a long day of work. Thankfully, he had picked up some takeout, so neither of us had to cook. While I was prepping our plates, Joe flipped on the TV and sank into the couch, football playing in the background. I felt a pang in my chest; we hadn't seen each other all day, and I was craving some real connection.

"Joe," I called out. "Can I talk to you about something?"

"Sure," he replied, eyes still on the screen.

I walked over and said, "I feel like we haven't really been connecting lately. You're always watching football, and I miss just . . . being with you."

His body tensed immediately. "What are you talking about?" he snapped. "I'm not always watching football. I just turned it on for a few minutes to unwind."

"I get that," I said, trying to stay calm, "But you've been in front of the TV a lot lately. It's starting to feel like we're drifting apart."

"What?! Oh, come on," he shot back. "I literally just turned it on. If I sit down for three minutes, it means I don't care about us? That we're not close?"

Then came the zinger: "What about you? You read your book in bed every night and don't even say good night half the time."

"That's different," I said, my voice rising. "I read to calm my mind so I can fall asleep. You, on the other hand, zone out for hours."

"So, it's okay for you to escape with a book, but if I watch a game, I'm the bad guy? That's not fair, Sarah. You're being a total hypocrite."

"Fine. Watch your game. I'm eating alone." I grabbed my plate and walked into the bedroom, shutting the door with more force than necessary. As I sat there eating, heart pounding, I started to reflect. Why had he reacted so strongly? What exactly was he defending?

That's when it hit me. Joe wasn't arguing about football. He was defending our closeness. My comment made him feel like he was failing me as a partner—and that landed right on his deepest fear: "I'm not enough." The irony? That same fear made him pull away from me, which only reinforced my feeling that we were drifting apart. I took a breath, walked back out to the living room, and softened my tone.

"Joe, can we hit reset for a minute?"

He paused the TV and looked over, clearly still a little raw.

"I'm sorry if I came across like I was attacking you. That wasn't

my intention. The truth is, I love you, and I do feel close to you. I just miss you. I was really hoping for some one-on-one time tonight. No distractions, just us."

Joe's posture softened. His voice lowered. "I get it. I really do. I'm sorry, too. We've both been running on empty lately. Putting some attention on each other is a good idea." He reached for the remote, hit record on the game, and then turned the TV off.

"I can watch it later," he said. "You matter more." I smiled and sat down close to him. We sat there, side by side on the couch, eating takeout and catching up—not about anything big, just sharing the little things we hadn't had time to say all week. In those small, ordinary moments, something shifted. The tension dissolved. The static between us cleared. We weren't trying to fix anything. We were just with each other. And that simple connection felt really, really good.

What's crazy is just how often this type of interaction occurs. While the subject matter might be different, the scenario is very common. When you can identify your man's fear of inadequacy beginning to surface, you can avoid fights going in circles. This is because you're able to spot the underlying need he is defending—his need to know that he is enough for you—which usually has nothing to do with the actual issue you're bringing up.

I'm not saying that his fear justifies getting defensive or critical. Your man is 100 percent responsible for how he responds to any given situation. And the more conscious a man is, the better he's able to receive your feedback or suggestions without it triggering his "I'm not enough" fear.

Perhaps there's a part of you that wishes your man would be the one to step up and apologize first. It's exhausting to feel like you have to be the emotionally aware one in moments like this. You're not wrong to want him to see it, own it, and step up. If you're always the one carrying the weight of the relationship, there's something bigger that needs fixing. Yet, none of us are perfect. There will always be times when one partner has more centeredness and awareness than the other. When that person is you, you are called to lead with love, not because it's your job to fix it, but because it's the most direct way back to the connection you truly want.

You may be thinking, *Does this mean I have to coddle a man?* Most certainly not. It's vital to speak up when you're frustrated and to voice your unmet expectations. It's *how* you communicate that makes all the difference. In chapter eleven, you'll learn highly effective strategies for giving him feedback and addressing challenges between you in such a way that he opens his heart rather than shutting it down.

But first, let's talk about something truly important: staying true to your standards.

Chapter Seven

Stay True to Your Standards

Rebecca met Derek on a Sunday morning at church. He was charming, handsome, and easy to talk to—the kind of guy who seemed to have his life together. They struck up a conversation after the service, and he quickly asked for her number. A few days later, he asked her out for coffee.

On their date, they clicked effortlessly. He was funny and attentive, and seemed genuinely interested in her. But as they wrapped up their lattes, Derek mentioned, almost offhandedly, that he had a girlfriend. A long-distance girlfriend.

Rebecca's heart sank. "Oh," she said, trying to keep her tone casual, "so you're still in a relationship?"

"Well, yes," he said, leaning back in his chair, "but it's not serious. We're on our way out. I'm planning to end it soon."

Rebecca took a slow breath, keeping her expression neutral. "Got it," she said. "Thanks for letting me know. But just so we're clear, I'm only interested in dating someone who's actually available. So if you do end things and you're truly single, feel free to reach out."

Derek nodded, his blue eyes holding hers. "I get it. And honestly, I want to be fully available for you. I'll handle it." A week later, Derek called and asked her to dinner. They went to a cozy Italian spot, the kind with twinkling string lights and checkered tablecloths. Halfway through the meal, Rebecca looked at him and asked, "So, did you break it off?"

Derek's jaw tensed. "Uhh, not yet," he said, stirring his pasta. "It's just . . . complicated. I was going to call her yesterday, but . . ."

There it was—the same old story. The same tired line. Rebecca placed her napkin on the table, her heart calm and steady. "Derek, you're a great guy," she said, leaning forward. "But I told you from the start, I'm only interested in dating someone who's fully available. I'm worth that, and honestly, so are you. When you're ready to walk your talk, maybe we can reconnect. Until then, take care."

She stood, slung her purse over her shoulder, and walked out, her head high and her heart intact. Because this time, she knew what she deserved.

That choice wasn't easy. But it was empowering. Staying true to your standards is an essential ingredient in creating attraction and shaping the overall quality of the relationship you want.

Three Steps to Staying True to Your Standards

Your standards are not a list of demands; they're a reflection of your self-worth. When you stay true to them, you send a powerful message to yourself and to the world: I know who I am, and I am worthy of what I desire and deserve.

Step One: Own Your Value

Owning your value means cherishing yourself and seeing yourself as someone who deserves to be fully loved, respected, and adored. It's not about arrogance or conceit, it's about recognizing that you are a woman who has innate worth, simply because you exist. It means believing—on a deep, cellular level—that your wants, needs, and desires matter.

When you own your value, you stop seeking approval or validation from others because you're already giving it to yourself. You no longer operate from a place of "this is good enough," whether you're dating or in a long-term relationship. Instead, you start choosing love rather than chasing it. You show up with the inner belief: I am worthy of the relationship I desire, and I'm creating it.

Owning your value is the foundation of staying true to your standards. Why? Because when you truly value yourself, you simply won't tolerate behavior that contradicts that value. You'll find yourself calmly walking away from situations that don't align with what you deserve—not out of anger, but out of self-respect. It's not about making someone else wrong; it's about honoring your own needs.

This practice looks like:

- Saying no to someone who consistently flakes on you, without feeling the need to justify or over-explain.
- Speaking up when something doesn't feel right, trusting that your voice matters and your perspective is valid.
- Walking away when you've done all you can and the relationship still isn't honoring your needs.

The beautiful thing about owning your value is that it automatically raises your standards, allowing you to attract a higher caliber of connection. It's like leveling up your love life because you're leveling up how you treat yourself. And the energy you radiate when you truly know your worth is magnetic, compelling, and irresistible.

An example of a woman who learned how to own her value is my client, Marissa. Marissa met Evan at a mutual friend's birthday party, and from the moment they started talking, sparks flew. Evan was handsome, fun, and attentive—the kind of guy who seemed genuinely interested in pursuing something real. Unlike many of the men she'd met before, Evan was open to a relationship. In fact, he made it clear he was looking for something serious.

But as their connection deepened, Marissa started to notice something was missing. While Evan was more than willing to spend time with her, their conversations never really went beneath the surface. Every attempt Marissa made to share her heart or dive into meaningful topics was met with lighthearted jokes, subject changes, or awkward silences. Evan wasn't a bad guy; he just didn't seem capable of the emotional depth Marissa craved.

Marissa knew she could keep dating him. After all, they had fun together. But fun wasn't enough. She was in a season of her life where she longed for a connection that felt rich, substantial, and deep. Someone who could hold space for her heart, not just make her laugh. So, even though Evan wanted a relationship, Marissa made the difficult but powerful decision to walk away. By choosing to end the relationship, Marissa sent a clear message to herself and the universe: "I am worthy of the love I desire, and I'm not afraid to let go of what's 'almost' to make space for what's aligned."

Step Two: Identify Your Standards

Once you're grounded in your value, it's time to get clear on your standards. Standards are your nonnegotiables, your deal-breakers, your love-life guardrails. They're based on your values and principles and define what you will and won't accept from others. This includes both the *negative* things you won't tolerate—like disrespect, dishonesty, emotional unavailability—as well as the *positive* things you require: love, presence, mutual support, consistency. Think of your standards as your personal relationship compass. Without them, it's easy to lose your way and fall into relationships that drain you rather than elevate you.

Examples of relationship standards might include:

- I will only commit to someone who is emotionally available and communicative.
- I will not tolerate being teased or emotionally manipulated.
- I require regular quality time and physical affection in a relationship.
- I will not rush physical intimacy before trust has been built.

You probably already have more standards than you realize. For example:

- As a single woman, you have a standard for who you'll give your number to.
- You have a standard for the kind of behavior that warrants a second date.
- You may have a standard for when you introduce someone to your children, your family, or your close friends.

In a long-term relationship, you have standards, too:

- How often you make time for connection and intimacy
- How you communicate during conflict
- How finances, parenting, or responsibilities are handled

Here's something important to remember—especially for single women: Sometimes holding your standard means *he might walk away*. And that's not a loss . . . that's a win. I can't tell you how many women I've coached who worried that if they asked a man to wait—for a second date, for exclusivity, or for sex—he'd lose interest. And here's what I always tell them: If a man doesn't want to wait, let him go.

You've got to be willing to scare off the wrong guy to attract the right guy. Because the right man—the one who honors you, values you, and wants something real—is not going to be turned off by your standards; he's going to be inspired by them. Holding to your standard doesn't repel quality men; it filters them *in*.

When you own your value, you don't bend yourself into a pretzel to keep someone's attention. You stand tall in your truth, trusting that anyone worth your time will *rise* to meet you there. And here's the beautiful part: your standards don't stop once you're in a relationship—they evolve. Because staying true to your standards isn't just about filtering in the dating phase; it's about maintaining the quality and vibrancy of your connection over time. When you speak your truth, you're not just asking for "more date nights" or "help with the kids," you're affirming your vision for the relationship.

My client Rachel realized that while her relationship had once been full of adventure, she and her partner had slowly slipped into a routine of work, parenting, and sleep. She decided to raise the standard. She asked her husband to plan one new shared experience a month—something fun, something spontaneous. Not only did he rise to the challenge, but he later told her it made him feel more alive, too. The key is *knowing* these standards consciously—so you can communicate them clearly.

Take a moment and reflect: What are your current standards? Which ones are super clear? Which ones are still fuzzy? What might need to be upgraded?

Your standards set the tone for your relationship. They're not just standards—they form the framework that supports how the two of you will be together and what experiences you co-create. The more clearly you define and share your standards, the more your relationship can thrive on mutual understanding, respect, and love.

Step Three: Speak Your Standards

This is where most people get stuck—not in *having* standards, but in *voicing* them. Speaking your standards isn't about giving ultimatums; it's about being self-honoring. It's choosing to advocate for your heart and your values with clarity, calmness, and confidence. When you express what matters to you, you show yourself (and others) that you are worth showing up for. Every time you speak a standard out loud, you tell yourself, "I matter," and that builds unshakable self-esteem. Too many women fear that voicing their needs will push a man away. But here's the thing: The *right* man isn't repelled by your standards—he's *inspired* by them.

Let me give you a real-life example from someone close to me—my stepbrother Michael. He and his wife, Isis, have a standard that's been a game changer for their connection: one date night every week, no exceptions. With three kids under the age of ten, life gets chaotic. Between football practice, homework, walking the dog, and grocery store marathons, their relationship can easily slip to the bottom of the priority list. That's why this standard isn't a "nice to have;" it's their lifeline.

But as life does, that standard got away from them. One missed date night turned into two, then a few skipped weeks, and pretty soon they hadn't had any true one-on-one time in almost a month. One Monday morning, Isis walked into the kitchen as Michael was sipping his coffee. She kissed him on the cheek, looked him in the eyes, and said gently but clearly, "Babe, I'm really missing my one-on-one time with you. Would you be willing to plan a date just for us this week—something romantic?"

Now, this wasn't a complaint. It wasn't a demand. It was a beautifully expressed standard, spoken with love and clarity. And it lit a fire in Michael. His masculine energy rose to the idea of providing her with something that she would love. She mattered, and he was all in.

That Friday night, Isis found herself sitting across from Michael at a candlelit table at Portland City Grill, high above the city skyline. The warm glow of the restaurant wrapped around them, and the hum of conversations faded into the background. She could see the city lights flickering below, but her attention was locked on the man in front of her, feeling so grateful for the one-on-one time she'd been craving. Halfway through the meal, she smiled, leaned in, and said softly, "Being out with you like this—just us—feels *so* good. It's like I can finally exhale." She reached across the table and took his hand. In that moment, Michael said it felt like he'd just won Olympic gold in the marriage event.

That's the power of a woman speaking her standards—not from pressure, but from presence. It gives your man a target he can hit, and nothing ignites healthy masculine energy more than a clear opportunity to win with the woman he loves.

This truth applies at *every* stage of the relationship, from longtime married couples to those just getting to know each other. Whether you've been together for fifteen years or fifteen minutes, speaking your standards is one of the most powerful ways to teach someone how to love you.

Let me give you one more story, from early in my relationship with my wife.

On our first date, Irene and I walked the Huntington Beach pier under the glow of a nearly full moon. It was breezy and romantic, and when I put my arm around her and we reached the end of the pier, I leaned in for what I thought was a guaranteed first-date kiss.

She smiled, gently pressed a finger to my lips, and said, "I'd *love* to kiss you right now. But I don't kiss on the first date."

My eyebrows lifted. "Seriously?"

She nodded. "Yep. Not on the first date. And besides, you don't even live here. I'm not sure how invested I want to get."

Her boundary surprised me. But it also *impressed* me. That was her standard. She stated it clearly and kindly, without apology. And instead of feeling rejected, I felt challenged . . . in a good way. We walked back down the pier hand in hand. And when we finally *did* kiss a few dates later, it was electric—not just because Irene is a phenomenal kisser (which she is), but because that kiss *meant* something. I had earned it. I had met her standard.

Since then, Irene has continued to own her value and speak her standards—whether it's needing more quality time, craving a day without the kids to recharge, or just wanting a long hug. And every time she does, she invites me into deeper connection with her. This is the beauty of staying true to your standards. You're not being high-maintenance. You're not being difficult. You're being *honest*. And honesty creates intimacy.

Don't shrink your needs. Don't silence your voice. Don't second-guess what you know you deserve. Instead:

- Own your value.
- Identify your standards.
- Speak your standards with confidence and love.

When you do, you don't just attract a relationship—you attract the *right* one. And if you're already in a relationship, you uplift it. You breathe life into it. You help keep it aligned with your vision for love—not just at the beginning, but for the long haul.

Hey, it's time for a little celebration! You've just cracked the first part of the man code: Igniting Attraction. Now, if you want to know what unlocks a man's heart and gives rise to even stronger feelings of love for you—the type of intense love that makes him want to swim an ocean, climb the highest mountain, or defeat 10,000 soldiers just to be by your side—that's exactly where we're headed in the next section: Deepening Connection.

Part Three

Deepening Connection

Chapter Eight

The Alchemy of Sex Drive

— Mr. Miami Goes to Seattle —

Candace checked her cell phone for what felt like the hundredth time that day. Still no text from Ben.

They had met online two weeks ago and spent a couple of evenings chatting on the phone. Candace had a good feeling about this guy, which only intensified when they met. On their first date, they'd gotten together for coffee and really hit it off. Almost immediately, she couldn't help but think about their possible future together. She had seen how easily Ben could fit into her life. She could picture their family vacations, and what the holidays would be like together. She even imagined how cute their kids would be.

Their second date the next Saturday had also been great—and steamy. The sex had been out of this world. Candace smiled just thinking about it.

The morning after, he'd texted, saying, "I had an amazing time. We should get together again. I'll call you soon."

But now it was already Friday and there had been no word since his Sunday message. *What a jerk*, she thought. Clearly their connection meant more to her than to him. Was he ever going to get back to her?

Sighing heavily, she flopped onto the couch and grabbed the remote, switching on the TV. Her eyes were on the screen, but her mind was elsewhere, replaying their time together. Her thoughts kept coming back to the same sad chorus: *We had such a great time. What happened? Did I do something wrong? Is there something wrong with me?*

If you've ever found yourself in a similar situation, asking some version of these same questions, this chapter is for you. In the following pages, you'll learn how a man deepens his emotions for you and ultimately falls in love—and the critical role sex plays in that process.

A quick heads-up: The majority of this chapter is most relevant to couples who are in the early stages of their relationship. If you're already in a committed relationship and enjoying sex with one another, then you're past the need for this material. Still, I think you'll find it fascinating and will likely want to share it with all the single women in your life.

We're about to explore where sex fits into the love equation for a man. I developed these concepts and analogies after having worked with tens of thousands of women over the last dozen years, and I offer them as a practical, time-tested approach to creating more emotional connection with your man.

So, make sure your How It Applies Spotlight is still turned on, and let's dive in.

— His Apartment Complex —

To get a picture of how a man falls in love, let's pop his hood, so to speak, and check out the inner workings of his brain. Though we live in the modern world, our brains still function much the same way they did thousands of years ago. And despite the fact that men's and women's brains are more alike than they are different, the differences in our sex drive and how we access our emotions are worth discussing, because they influence how we fall in love.

Consider this fun analogy I've developed over the years to help women understand how a man's mind works: Imagine that his brain operates like a giant apartment complex. In other words, his brain is "apartmentalized."

Each apartment in his brain is dedicated to one topic or activity in his life. For example, he has an apartment for work. He has a different apartment for his relationship with you. He's got an apartment for his hobbies. An apartment for exercise. You name it, there's a separate apartment for it. This system helps him focus more deeply on whatever it is he's engaged in. The main drawback to this arrangement is that he can only be in one apartment at a time.

Ever wonder why he can't hear you or struggles to maintain a conversation when he's watching TV? Most women, who are pros at multitasking, find this hard to understand, but it's not because he's "dim-witted" or doesn't love you. It's just how his brain works: when he's in his TV-watching apartment, his conversation abilities are located down the hall in a completely separate apartment!

The other important aspect of a man's apartmentalized brain is the priority his sex apartment receives—as if it's a giant penthouse! Not kidding. Research shows that the area of the brain associated with sexual pursuit is significantly larger in men than in women.[16] Plus, men have around fifteen times more testosterone than women (the hormone that's primarily responsible for sex drive for both men and women).[17] The person who said the way to a man's heart was through his stomach was definitely aiming too high!

Granted, you may want sex just as much (if not more) than the man in your life. If that's you, more power to you! There are no "right" or "wrong" levels of sex drive. We are all our own individuals. The point is, in new relationships, you can help your man convert some of his sexual energy into emotional connection if you know how the alchemy of sex drive works.

— Miami Versus Seattle —

The first step in creating an emotional connection is knowing how to help your man get from his sex apartment to his relationship apartment—the space that houses his commitment level and emotional connection to you.

To start, it's important to understand that in our analogy of a man's apartmentalized brain, his relationship apartment is nowhere near his penthouse sex apartment. It's as if it's located on the opposite side of the complex. In fact, these two "apartments" are so far apart that traveling from one to the other is like journeying from Miami (his sex apartment) to Seattle (his relationship apartment).

This Miami–Seattle chasm presents a unique challenge for a man getting into a new relationship because the more attracted to you he is, the more likely he'll be starting out in his Miami apartment. Though he may be hoping he'll develop powerful feelings for you, until he visits his Seattle apartment he won't know for sure.

A woman's brain is a completely different story. Speaking again in analogies, it doesn't operate like an apartment complex, but rather like an internet superhighway—where every topic is linked to every other topic in your life. Your relationship is linked to your job, which is linked to your friendships, which is linked to your finances, which is linked to your health, which is linked to your family, which is linked to your travel, which is linked to sex, which is linked back to your relationship, and so on. Like an internet browser, you can easily keep all these topics open on different tabs, clicking back and forth between them with incredible deftness, thinking about twenty-seven items in a fraction of a second. Plus, not only can you rapidly switch between tabs, but you're working with a high-speed emotional connection that gives you the ability to understand how you feel about any given topic the moment you click on it.

These differences don't mean that men feel their emotions less deeply than women do. Men feel their emotions just as intensely as women. The difference is the role sex plays in how we generate a deeper emotional connection with each other.

For women, whose "tabs" are all interconnected, more often than not, jumping in the sack with a guy emotionally bonds her to him and acts like a high-speed love magnifier. Even the woman who wants to keep things "casual"—if she isn't careful and has too many amazing nights with Mr. Sexy—can find that every tab she clicks on has his smiling face on it! She's doing the one thing she swore she wouldn't do—"fall for him"—due in part to the fantastic orgasm-induced oxytocin bath she's receiving.

Whereas for men, having sex and reaching orgasm—which happens to be his favorite activity when he's in "Miami"—does *not* bond him emotionally to you. Remember, his relationship apartment (which contains his commitment level and emotional bond) is located across the metaphorical country in Seattle!

This helps explain why you might be faster at knowing how you feel about wanting a committed relationship than your man. You can simply tab back and forth to understand your emotions, while your man needs to take a metaphorical flight from his Miami apartment to his Seattle apartment.

If you don't understand this difference in emotional timing, it's easy to get frustrated or think something's wrong—especially if his feelings don't seem to match the way you're feeling in the beginning. Plus, in a new relationship, it's scary when you put your heart on the line and the other person doesn't confirm that they share the same emotions.

That's when most women pull back. They shut down their emotions and think perhaps that being together isn't meant to be. This is also when a man may be tempted to end the relationship. Not because he doesn't like you, but because he's scared that he's going to hurt you if, by the time he gets to his Seattle apartment, he realizes that he doesn't feel the same way you do.

Remember, a healthy masculine man's instinct is to protect you, even if that means breaking up sooner, to avoid hurting you even more down the line.

But just because he hasn't "gotten there emotionally" by the time you have doesn't mean he won't arrive. It's quite possible while you've already clicked back and forth between what you want, how he measures up, and how you feel about him more than a hundred times, he still hasn't left his Miami apartment.

Of course, you may have had experiences with guys who were emotionally invested before you were. They fell in love with you quickly and were ready to commit while you were still making up your mind. These men were likely already looking for a relationship, which means they started in their Seattle apartment. They met you and immediately saw how wonderful life with you in "Seattle" could be. They chose you as their person, committed their hearts to you, and fell in love!

But how do you know if the guy you've just met is in his Miami apartment? And if he is, how can you help him visit Seattle?

— Sexual Pacing and Emotional Pacing —

The best evidence that your man has visited his Seattle apartment and has developed a deeper emotional connection with you is when he asks you to be exclusive with him. Which means, if the guy you're dating hasn't committed to you and voiced that he's falling in love with you, then a good rule of thumb is to simply assume that he's hanging out in his Miami apartment.

If you want to inspire a man to take a trip to Seattle where he'll access and expand his deeper emotions for you, here's a two-part formula that has been highly effective for many of my clients.

Part One: Let him set the emotional pace for the relationship, while you set the sexual pace.

The emotional pace refers to the level of commitment you're both willing to make to the relationship. The sexual pace refers to your level of sexual activity, from kissing to lovemaking. In a new relationship, it can be quite a shock to a woman who's been sleeping with a guy for several weeks when she asks him, "Sooo, what are we?" or "Where do you see this going?" and he doesn't have a clear answer!

She assumes he must not care about her, when in reality, he just doesn't know exactly what his commitment level is yet. He hasn't been to his Seattle apartment because things are so darn good in Miami. Remember, unless he's motivated to visit his Seattle apartment (and check out his commitment level and how he feels about this relationship), he's as happy as a clam to hang out in his Miami apartment and enjoy the hot connection you have together.

This brings us to the second half of the formula . . .

Part Two: Make sure the emotional pace of the relationship leads the sexual pace.

Since you're in charge of how fast you go sexually, there are two very important words you need to know that are crucial for setting the sexual pace and that will transform his sexual energy into emotional connection and help him fall in love with you even faster.

Those words are "NOT YET." In other words, "Nope, I'm not gonna have sex with you until you meet my standards, big guy." Now, before you slam this book shut and throw it across the room, yelling, "Mat, this isn't the 1950s. I have needs, too!" let me explain. You're not saying "no" forever; you're simply saying not until the relationship is at the commitment level you want it to be to sleep together. Remember, you're the one who decides what prerequisites need to be met before having sex. This one simple, yet powerful, move harnesses your man's potent sex drive and combines it with his masculine instinct to provide what you want—all of which causes him to start fueling up his proverbial jet—next stop, Seattle!

But first, how do you determine your standards for sex? Well, it starts by deciding what kind of relationship you want. Do you want to get married? Do you want to date lots of people? Do you want a meaningful long-term partnership with someone? Do you just want a friend with benefits?

Some women want to save sex until marriage. Nothing wrong with that. Some women want to have sex on the first date. That's okay, too. All you need to do is simply match your standards for sex with the type of relationship you want to experience. If you want to keep things casual or have a friend with benefits, then as long as you both agree, go for it.

If your goal is to build an emotionally committed and exclusive relationship with a man, then wait to have sex until you *already* have that type of relationship. A lot of women believe that having sex is the way to create that relationship, but it doesn't usually work that way.

Remember, sex is the most physically intimate thing you can do with each other. So, reserving sex until the relationship meets your standards motivates your man to answer this fundamental question: "How do I *really* feel about her?" And ensures you're only sleeping with someone who has a quality answer to that question.

There's another reason why reserving sex until he's committed to you is so effective at helping him fall in love: his instinct to conserve energy. Since men can only be in one apartment at a time, without some significant internal or external motivator, he has no reason to go to his Seattle apartment. If you sleep together right away, he's content to kick back, put his feet up, and chill right there in his Miami apartment.

I call this the "sex-fog." As crazy as it sounds, a man can go months dating you, sleeping with you, and still not have a clear answer as to how he really feels about you and whether he wants something longer term. When a man is in the sex-fog, all planes are grounded, and there are no flights from Miami to Seattle.

Now, if you're down to keep things casual and don't prefer a commitment at this point in your life, then the two of you can have a blast in his Miami apartment, and there's no need for him to travel to his Seattle apartment.

On the other hand, if you want commitment and/or a deeper

emotional connection with him, then saying "not yet" helps him convert all that pent-up sexual energy into jet fuel and gives him the motivation he needs to do his emotional discovery.

— Mr. Miami Goes to Seattle —

Let's peek at a dating example and see how and when to apply the pacing formula so that you don't end up ghosted like Candace, whom you met at the beginning of the chapter.

Imagine this scenario: You connect with a great guy online and have a couple of nice phone conversations together. He's smart, funny, kind, and attractive, with a great job. Plus, he follows through and calls you when he says he will.

The two of you decide to meet at a restaurant for a dinner date. When he sees you walk up to the front door, you notice the damn-she's-hot gleam in his eyes. He thinks you look even better than your pictures. He feels a wave of excitement travel up and down his entire body. He's definitely sexually attracted to you (which means he's hunkered down in his Miami apartment—probably grooving to some Barry White!). At the same time, you find him extremely attractive. You feel butterflies swirling in your stomach because you know he's got potential.

The conversation easily flows the entire dinner. You're both laughing and enjoying the conversation, as you discover all the things you have in common. After dinner, he invites you back to his place for a drink. Feeling the rising sexual tension between you, a part of you is screaming, *Yes, yes, yes!* but another part of you knows that any deepening of connection at this moment would probably be "skin-deep" and just for the night. You are looking for a committed relationship, so you decide to politely decline, but you let him know you'd love to see him again.

He asks you out for the next weekend. You two text or talk on the phone every day leading up to the date. This time it's a Saturday afternoon date for an activity you love. You're both feeling even more attraction for each other. He's a total gentleman, listening, sharing, and being considerate. Again, he can't take his eyes off you. The two of you are obviously flirting and really enjoying each other's company. After your spectacular afternoon together, you invite him back to your place to continue the "conversation."

Inevitably, things start to heat up. You're kissing on the couch, and he feels *really* good to you. He then invites you to move things into the bedroom. While your body wants to rip his clothes off, your mind knows the two of you are still getting to know each other. It's early in the relationship and your standards for sex haven't been met yet. You want to communicate your standards to him, while at the same time, you don't want to push him away because you really like this guy. What can you say?

Here's a powerful technique you can use that communicates your standards *and* activates the Alchemy of Sex Drive:

Step 1: Affirm your attraction
Step 2: State your standards
Step 3: Give him the opportunity to rise to the challenge (no pun intended!)

Whenever a man suggests getting more physically intimate than you're comfortable with, you can simply say:

1. **(Affirm your attraction)** "You have no idea how much I want you right now."
2. **(State your standards)** "And I'm saving sex for when [fill in the blank with your standard] ______________________."

Examples of standards are "When I'm in an exclusive and committed relationship with someone" or "When I've spent more time with someone, and we've committed to building something special together."

Here's an example of how the first statements go together: "You have no idea how much I want you right now, and I'm saving that for when I'm in an exclusive and committed relationship."

Here's an important nuance: Your man wants to know that you share his mutual attraction. So make sure to use the word "and" instead of "but" when you state your standards. The word "but" erases the meaning of your previous statement where you affirm your attraction for him.

Any statement that goes "I'm attracted to you, but . . ." is interpreted as "I'm not really attracted to you." On the other hand, using the word "and" allows the meaning of the previous statement to carry forward. Yes, you are attracted to him, *and* your standards haven't been met yet.

3. **(Give him the opportunity to rise to the challenge)** "As much as I'd love to say yes, we're not there yet."

Using this formula motivates your man to answer a very important question. "Do I have what it takes to deliver what she wants?"

Back to our imaginary date—and the couch. He asks you to move things into the bedroom, and you use that formula:

"You have no idea how much I want you right now. *And* I'm saving that for when I'm in an exclusive and committed relationship. As much as I'd love to say yes, we're not there yet." Though you both feel the sexual tension at an all-time high, he respects your wishes, and you finish the date with a wonderful, sensual kiss goodbye.

Because you've spoken your standards, he now knows that if he's going to ask you out again, having sex is not on the table. (Figuratively or literally!) If he asks you for another date, it will have to be because he's growing the kind of feelings for you that would make him want to be exclusive and eventually commit to this relationship. All of that sexual desire now fuels his "jet" as he prepares to fly at supersonic speed from "Miami" to "Seattle."

[Audio crackles] Hello there, this is your captain speaking. Welcome aboard! The fog has lifted, and we've been cleared for takeoff. Please fasten your seat belt and make sure your tray table is in its full, upright, and locked position. Our next stop, the gorgeous city of Seattle. Enjoy your flight . . .

When he skids into his Seattle apartment, he has significant motivation to answer the five primary questions that help him know if this is a relationship he wants to pursue. Here are the five most important questions he explores:

1. How do I feel about her?
2. How do I feel about myself when I'm around her?
3. Is this what I want at this stage in my life?
4. Do I have what it takes to make her happy?
5. Can I see myself with her long-term?

He needs to get a positive response to all five of these questions before he's willing to commit to growing this relationship with you.

Once he gets positive answers to these questions, the sexual desire he has for you will intensify the emotional connection he feels. That's why I call it the Alchemy of Sex Drive. Look, are there couples who have slept together on the first date and now have a long-lasting, happy marriage? Yes, indeed. But that's not the common experience.

After working with tens of thousands of women over the last decade, I've found that it's way more likely after sleeping together on the first date that a man will stop pursuing her. He started in his Miami apartment. He shared a beautiful sexual experience with her—received what he was pursuing—and because he hadn't visited his Seattle apartment, he didn't have the emotional engagement to pursue a relationship with her beyond sex.

If you're the type of person who's simply interested in a sexual relationship, then that strategy will work well. If you're getting the result you want, then stay the course. However, if you're not getting the result you want, know there's an opportunity to help both of you bond on a deeper level by transforming the sexual energy into emotional connection.

In fact, if a man learns about the Alchemy of Sex Drive, he can apply it to himself to open his heart and build a stronger connection. This is exactly what happened to one of my good friends. I met Dan at the gym when we both kept showing up for our workouts at 7 AM sharp. He was a hard guy to miss. In his late thirties, Dan looked like a modern-day Superman: a head of thick dark hair, deep blue eyes, a chiseled jaw, and a broad, muscular chest. On top of that, he was mega-successful. A few years earlier, he had started his own marketing firm, and it was going gangbusters.

Dan and I hit it off, chatting between dead lifts and squats, eventually expanding our friendship beyond the gym to play basketball and go surfing together. As we shot hoops or sat on our boards waiting for waves, we talked about business, life, my relationship with Irene, and his sex-capades—of which there were many.

One day as we floated in the ocean, watching the surf, I asked him, "How was your date with Rachel last night?"

He blew out his breath in a loud sigh. "Pretty much like all of them."

"What do you mean?" I asked.

"Well, the only thing Rachel and all the other women I go out with seem to want is to jump into the sack on our first date."

I made a scoffing sound. "Cry me a river, dude."

He gave me a wry smile. "Hey, don't get me wrong, the hookups are really fun, but, Mat, I've been doing this for years and I'm getting tired of it. I'm just not able to connect my heart to any of these women, and our dates never seem to develop into anything. I feel like I'm ready for a real relationship. I want someone special to share my life with."

He turned to face me, and I saw the longing in his eyes as he asked, "You and Irene made it happen and seem really good together. How did you get there?"

"You really want to know?" I said. "I'm not sure a sex-positive guy like you is going to like it."

He said, "Try me!" So I shared the "Miami–Seattle" principle with him, suggesting he use the Alchemy of Sex Drive on himself by simply telling these women "no sex" until he felt there was enough emotional connection to become exclusive.

He got a pained expression on his face. "Ooh, that's gonna be tough!"

I laughed. "Yup, believe me, I know!"

But Dan wanted a different result and was committed to trying something new. So, over the next few weeks, Dan stuck to his guns, letting the women he dated know that he was reserving sex for someone he wanted a committed relationship with.

Then, as so often happens, we both got busy. I went on a couple out-of-town business trips and Dan's business required extra hours, so we didn't hang out for more than a month.

One night, I got a two-word text from Dan: "It worked!"

I called him and asked, "What worked?"

He was pumped. "The Alchemy of Sex Drive, that's what! I finally went to my Seattle apartment. My heart is open like it's never been open before. I'm totally falling in love with this woman. I think she's the one!"

A year later, Irene and I sat together holding hands at Dan and Samantha's wedding. Although we were in Southern California, Dan's smile was so bright, I wouldn't doubt it could be seen all the way to Miami!

Did Dan wait for his wedding day to have sex? Not even close. But he did wait long enough to form a strong emotional bond and commit to being exclusive with Samantha. Dan's built-up sexual energy acted like Miracle-Gro, nourishing the budding emotional connection he had with her. For Dan, it was just what he needed to help him fall in love.

You may resonate with Dan's story. In which case, you may consider giving yourself the same prescription to help you open your heart. Or, you may be thinking, *Does that mean "no messing around" until he's met my standards, or we're in a committed relationship?* For you, that might be taking it a little too far. Again, I'm a fan of tools, not rules. The spirit of this principle is to help your man go to his Seattle apartment, so that he can get in touch with his feelings for you.

In fact, kissing and messing around can be a good thing, as they fuel his metaphorical tanks, building the sexual tension between you. But if you take him to the top of his mountain before he's committed to you and he spends all his fuel in Miami (wink, wink), he might not be taking a flight to Seattle anytime soon.

— Keep the Sex Train Moving —

The Alchemy of Sex Drive is a beautiful process in the beginning of a relationship to help your man build an emotional connection and fall in love with you. But after you form a committed relationship and have gotten that sex train running, make sure to keep it on the tracks. Why? Because, once he's met your standard for sleeping together and he's committed to a relationship with you, having sex helps strengthen the emotional bond between you and fuels the love you have for one another.

If you want to keep your romance juicy, having sex is vital. It's the single biggest factor that distinguishes a romantic relationship from a friendship. If the sex dies, then the romantic relationship begins to die. The couples who thrive together are the ones that prioritize lovemaking.

Now, chances are, one of you will probably want sex more than the other—which can be uncomfortable and emotionally painful. One person feels bad because they're usually saying no, and the other person consistently feels rejected. However, the couples who are the most connected do their best to lean in and accommodate one another, even when they aren't feeling revved up. They find quick ways to get themselves from zero to "ready," so to speak, so they can get it on—because they know how valuable sex is, not just for their partner, but for the overall relationship. They also understand that intercourse is only one way to get sexual with your partner, and they're willing to explore other ways to pleasure each other.

Still, as we get older, both men and women can face physical limitations, as well as other challenges in the bedroom. But don't give up hope, because with good communication, problem-solving skills, and a healthy sense of humor, you can find ways to keep the sex hot for "as long as you both shall live"! Take it from me, I heard *a lot* about this in the many personal interviews I had with couples in their eighties and nineties!

Bottom line, whether you've just decided to become intimate with each other, or you've been married for decades, keep that sex train rolling, because lovemaking contains a powerful energy that makes the fires of attraction blaze while significantly deepening your emotional connection.

GIFTBOX

Want some great tips on how to touch your man in ways that will drive him wild? Go here.

Chapter Nine

The Ultimate Connection Code

— What His Heart Longs For —

The room was heavy with tension. Fifty men sat in a line of identical chairs, each holding a clipboard. In front of us stood fifty women, eyes large and expectant, waiting for instructions. None of us knew what was coming.

The facilitator stepped forward, a woman in her seventies dressed head-to-toe in purple, her gaze sharp and commanding. "Ladies, you're going to play a game called 'The Island Game.' Here's the question you'll be answering for each man in front of you: If he were the last man on the planet, would you want to be stranded with him on a deserted island? Yes, or no?"

The instructions hit me like a punch to the gut. The women began to move down the line, locking eyes with each man and giving their unfiltered answers. "Yes." "No." "No." "Yes."

I tried to keep my composure as the votes for or against me rolled in. Some women said yes, but many more said no. When the exercise was over, the facilitator asked us to line up based on our scores—from the most "yes" votes to most "no" votes. As I took my place, my heart sank. I was nearly at the end of the line. Only one guy had received more "no" votes than me—and he was someone who made my skin crawl, the loud and abrasive type. That realization hit me like a freight train. How had I become so unapproachable?

The facilitator scanned the line. "Mat, would you be open to receiving feedback?" I swallowed hard. My ego screamed to run, to defend myself, but deep down, I knew I needed to hear it.

I nodded. "Yes."

One by one, the women shared their impressions. "You're hiding emotionally." "You come off as guarded." "It's hard to connect with the real you." Their words stung, but they also resonated. For years, in an attempt to create connection, I'd been desperately trying to look good, to impress others, to keep my flaws hidden. But instead of drawing people closer, my self-criticism and emotional walls had created an energy that pushed them away.

That night, as I lay in bed, tears streaming down my face, I finally admitted to myself that I had no idea how to create the connection I craved. I found myself unable to stop thinking about it. I could still feel the humiliation of getting so many no votes; the reasons the women had given swirled in my mind.

"You have walls up . . ."

"I can't connect to the 'real' you . . ."

"It feels like you're only showing me the parts of yourself that you want me to see . . ."

"You're hiding emotionally . . ."

"I feel judged, like I can't be my true self around you . . ."

In my heart, I knew they were spot on. I *wasn't* letting people in, I *was* hiding, and although I wasn't judging others, I was judging *myself*—hard! In fact, I was so self-critical that I radiated a general vibe of judgment. And no one wants to be around that kind of negative judging energy.

Painfully aware that my "you-have-to-look-good-to-others" mentality and hiding my faults to avoid rejection was sabotaging the love and connection I so deeply wanted, I knew I needed to fix this. I had to learn to love and accept myself, warts and all. The problem was I had no idea how to start.

The day after my return, my long-time friend Angela called. She knew I'd been attending a transformational seven-day seminar aimed at discovering anything holding me back in my love life. She was eager to hear any insights I'd gained.

I had mixed feelings. I wanted to talk to her about what had happened but was also terrified to tell her what the women had said. My desire to share with my friend won out, and I invited her to stop by that evening.

At 7 PM on the dot, the doorbell rang. Still unsure of what to say, I opened the door. Angela greeted me with a warm smile and wrapped her arms around me, giving me a big bear hug.

"Welcome back!" she said, and walked past me to the couch, expectant and excited to hear all about my adventures in personal growth–land. "Sooo . . . tell me all about it. How was the retreat?"

I sat down next to her, my stomach roiling over how much to reveal.

"Really great," I said flatly, clearly in my head. "Lots of . . . uhhh, deep insights."

"*Okaaay*, like what?" she probed. "Tell me, I want to hear."

I sat for a moment, my eyes downcast, debating with myself, *Should I tell her? What if she laughs at me or thinks I'm weak? Or worse yet, gets angry that I've put on a looking-cool persona with her all this time? What if she doesn't want to be my friend anymore?* Anguished, I raised my head and took in Angela's loving smile. *Ah, screw it!* I thought, *I'm just gonna tell her . . .*

I took a deep breath, and for the first time in what felt like a lifetime, I didn't hold back. I told Angela everything: being voted second to last on the Island Game, how utterly embarrassed I felt, the harsh, yet brilliant, feedback the women had given me, my fear of rejection and pushing people away by trying to "be perfect" all the time—my constant self-criticism, and so on.

It was hard to look at Angela while I spoke. I spent much of the time looking down at my hands, fearing what her facial expressions might reveal. When I finished, I finally looked up. Angela's eyes glistened with tears as she took my hands in hers. "Mat," she said, "I want you to know I have never felt closer to you than I do right now. What you shared is so beautiful and brave. You say you want connection, well . . . being open and showing others who you really are is how you get it. Because the truth is, we're all scared, we all want connection. Thank you, thank you, thank you for sharing that with me."

Hearing her words, something tense and tight melted inside me. Angela said she felt closer to me than ever before, and to my surprise, I realized *I* felt closer to *her* than ever before, too. A new sense of freedom washed over me. I had accepted myself enough to share my story with Angela, and for the first time I felt free to be my authentic self.

Angela's words pointed the way forward: The more I could love and accept myself, flaws and all, the more I'd be able to share myself fully, leading to more love and connection with others.

— The Ultimate Connection Code —

What do all human beings want? Across every culture, at every age, from every corner of the globe, we all crave the same thing—to be loved and accepted. When someone feels loved and accepted by you, they feel free to be themselves around you. They can open their hearts, experience their emotions more deeply, and express who they really are with you. This feeling of acceptance is essential to their sense of well-being, and it's the anchor that grounds their connection with you.

The lesson I learned from the Island Game is that you cannot give something to someone that you yourself don't have. While I know that might sound cliché, really understanding that lesson deeply was the catalyst to opening my heart. If I wanted to experience more meaningful connection in my life, then I had to first stop being so self-critical and learn how to accept and love myself for who I was, including all my flaws. Only then could I offer that same acceptance to someone else and build the true connection I desired. Self-love was one of the essential keys I needed for relationship success.

If you want to create a phenomenal connection with your partner, then your partner must feel that you're able to accept them for who they are. And the place this begins is by first loving and accepting yourself for who you are. When you're radiating self-judgment and self-criticism, the people around you pick up on these vibrations and a part of their deeper psyche thinks you might turn that same judgment on them. When your energy softens, your man instinctively feels that same energy of acceptance extend to him.

Once he experiences that acceptance, he feels safe to share his feelings and innermost thoughts with you—from his deepest desires to his hidden worries, as well as his goofy, playful side. And as you accept more of yourself, you'll also feel freer to open up and show him more of who you really are. And it's when you both feel free and safe to be yourselves—sharing your fears, your needs, and your desires with each other—that the greatest levels of closeness and connection are created.

Granted, I know accepting and loving yourself fully might sound like a tall order. Frankly, it kinda is. It's not something that happens overnight, but it gets easier with daily practice. The good news is, you don't have to be perfect at accepting yourself to create more authentic connection in your relationship.

— The Three Connection Keys —

Although there are entire books written on the topic of self-love, throughout my journey I've found three practices (or keys) that when used regularly create a phenomenal energy of acceptance for yourself *and* your man that will anchor a powerful bond between you.

Connection Key One: Love the Unloved

The first key helps reverse any old habits you may have of self-judgment and beating yourself up. I first learned this practice from one of my mentors, Dr. Gay Hendricks, and have since shared it with thousands of clients over the years. The best part is, it isn't hard to master.

The point of this key is to practice loving the parts of yourself that you don't like, want to change, or wish were different. You may be thinking, *Mat, if I could love those parts then I would, but there's a reason I don't love them. They're embarrassing and terrible.* I understand. But bear with me because there are two reasons this process works so well.

First, to accept yourself, you simply love yourself as you are—even the part of you that *doesn't* love yourself! This works because love is greater than any other emotion you can feel. It's greater than fear, greater than shame, greater than sadness, anger, regret, guilt—you name it, love is more powerful than that. Love is even greater than the resistance to loving yourself. So, no matter what you're feeling, love can transform it.

Second, you don't have to be perfect at this process to gain major benefits. In fact, not being perfect is, in and of itself, perfect. Releasing the demand for perfection is at the core of this acceptance practice. So even if you think you're not doing the practice perfectly, simply love and accept yourself for not being perfect and you'll begin to experience the benefits.

This practice can start to deliver results right away. But even if you don't consciously notice any changes, stick with it—over time you'll begin to feel significant improvement in your relationship with yourself and others.

Here's how it works:

1. Start by releasing any expectation or attachment to the way

you're supposed to feel during this process. Give yourself permission to simply engage in this process and accept whatever occurs—as it is.

2. Close your eyes and take a few slow, easy, deep breaths. When you're feeling relaxed, ask yourself one of these questions: "What in me needs my love and acceptance right now?" Or "What parts of myself do I have trouble loving and accepting just as they are?" Notice what answers come to you. Whatever arises, imagine connecting to your heart's energy and sending a warm beam of love from your heart to the place in you that needs your love and acceptance.
3. Silently say to yourself, "I fully and completely love and accept this part of me now." Allow the part of you that needs your love and acceptance to relax. Use your imagination and see this part of you embraced and enfolded by your loving beam of energy. Feel this part of you absorbing the loving energy. Stay with this experience for at least thirty seconds.
4. Take three slow, deep breaths and stay with the feeling of love for as long as you want.
5. To close this process, place your hand over your heart and silently say to yourself, "I fully and completely love and accept myself now."
6. Take one final deep breath and slowly open your eyes. Allow this feeling of love to be with you as you move through your day.

It's super important not to judge yourself on whether you're doing the practice right, but to simply accept whatever your experience is. Some days you'll feel the love more intensely, some days you'll feel it less intensely; whatever you feel, just let it be and accept it as it is.

As you integrate the practice of self-love into your daily life, pay special attention to those moments when you make a mistake. Instead of condemning or berating yourself (which is what most people do), give yourself a break and offer yourself more love in that moment.

As you're softer on yourself, you'll be able to be softer on your man when he falls short. Which leads us straight to our second connection key.

Connection Key Two: Be a Soft Place to Fall

The depth of your connection with your man isn't just the result of the time you spend together but is determined by the quality of that time. Deep connection is often created in micro-moments—specific opportunities that you seize to forge an even stronger bond with each other.

One of the most magical opportunities to forge this stronger connection is when your partner makes a mistake, because when a person makes a mistake, it puts them in an emotionally vulnerable—and more open—state. In that state, your partner will register your criticism or your compassion more deeply, depending on how you choose to handle that moment.

We all make mistakes—like accidentally knocking over a glass of red wine at a party, forgetting someone's birthday, or one of my personal bests: being on a 6 AM radio show during my first book tour in Dallas and saying on air how excited I was to be in Denver. Oh yes, because nothing says "media savvy" like getting the city wrong on a book tour. Every one of us has had those "crawl-into-a-hole" moments after a blunder.

However, when our partners make mistakes, it's easy to miss these opportunities to create connection, because most of us do what was likely done to us—we criticize and blame the person who made the mistake.

If, instead of criticizing or blaming, you become "a soft place to fall" for your man—in other words, you offer understanding and compassion—then you protect his heart when he's feeling exposed rather than attacking it. This creates an enormous emotional impact he won't soon forget. I'm not suggesting you condone bad behavior or excuse your man for shirking his responsibilities. I'm talking about the moments when he owns what happened, feels bad about it, and can't change the result. Being a soft place to fall at those times is incredibly powerful for strengthening your connection.

I learned the power of this firsthand, thanks to my wife—who, in one of my most humiliating early marriage moments, became a soft place to fall. I've never forgotten it (and doubt I ever will). To this day, I'm profoundly moved by her response.

It was the day after our wedding. Irene and I sat together on the floor of our tiny apartment's living room, opening our wedding presents. Irene's smile still glowed from our wedding day as she considered where to place these items in our new home. Irene was asking me whether I wanted to open the big silver box or a small pink present next when a ping from my phone interrupted her. The text read, "Your flight leaves in one hour."

No, that can't be! I thought, *we're flying out for our honeymoon tomorrow, not today.* Irene had trusted me to book the honeymoon, and I was certain I booked our flight for the next day.

Seeing the blood drain out of my face, she asked, "Is everything okay?"

"Uh, yeah, I think so. Let me go check something." I ran to the desk in my office and logged on to my computer. *Sh*t! You've gotta be FU%KING kidding me!*

The text was correct. Our flight to Cancun was leaving in fifty-two minutes. I'd totally blown it. How could I mess up the flight to our freaking honeymoon?! I looked into rebooking the flight for later that day. The earliest flight available was the next day and would cost an additional $1,500, cutting into our already tight budget. Ouch, but I booked it anyway. Next, I called the hotel. Although they wouldn't give us our money back for the night, they did allow us to check in the following day.

Okay, now to tell Irene. I felt my stomach turn inside out with embarrassment. The sound of Irene happily singing as she put presents away made me wince. *How do I break this news to her?* My heart pounded as I walked into the room. She stopped putting away our things and looked over at me.

"What's up?" she asked.

"I made a mistake, babe," I replied, rubbing my forehead, still dumbfounded at how I could have screwed this up.

"Okay, what happened?"

"Well, you know how I said our flight to Cancun was tomorrow? It's actually today. In fact, it leaves thirty minutes from now. We won't make it. I totally blew it."

"Oh no," she said as she looked at me. I could feel her mental wheels turning as she waited for more information.

"But . . . we do have a new flight for tomorrow morning. It cost fifteen hundred dollars to make the change, but we can use our wedding money. And I called the hotel; our reservation is still good. It will just be one day shorter. I'm really, *really* sorry, honey. I totally screwed this up," I said, shaking my head and looking down at the floor.

"Hang on, I need to grab something from the kitchen," Irene said as she walked quickly out of the room. Not knowing if she was going to come back with a tissue in her hand to wipe tears that were surely welling in her eyes, or with a knife she was going to use to kill me . . . I waited.

After a few moments, she returned, took a deep breath, and paused. She could see how embarrassed I was to have cost us an entire day of our honeymoon. She walked over and held my hands.

"That's okay, babe," she said. "We don't need to be in Cancun to start our honeymoon. We can start our honeymoon right here, right now." Then she reached up and took my face in her hands. Looking at me with loving eyes, she kissed me, and said, "Tomorrow we'll board that plane, and we'll have a great time."

Her understanding melted my shame and embarrassment. She could have easily attacked me with daggers of criticism, saying things like, "How could you not remember the date of our flight? Why didn't you put a reminder on? Doesn't our honeymoon mean anything to you?" But instead, she held my emotions in her loving hands and became a soft place to fall.

I scooped her up, carrying her into the bedroom, and we started our honeymoon right then. Our trip to Cancun was indeed magical. But what

I remember most is how my wife protected my heart when it would have been easy to rake me over the coals. For that, I am eternally grateful.

This is not to say that you must be perfect at being a soft place to fall all the time. None of us are perfect. In fact, Irene told me later that when she walked into the kitchen during our talk, she felt a rush of heat through her body as she had a freak-out moment, silently screaming, *Oh. My. God! How could he forget what day our flight was?!* But after a few seconds, she thought to herself, *Well, I didn't check to see what day our flight was either.* Calming down a little more, she had another thought: *If I'd done this, how would I want Mat to respond to me?* Taking a long, slow breath, she returned to where she'd left me, ready to be as understanding as she'd want me to be if the tables were turned.

When you see your man has made a mistake and he's attempted to make it right, see it as more than just a misstep. Seize it as a sacred opportunity. In that moment, your compassion has the power to become a healing force. Your softness becomes strength. And your response becomes a memory he'll carry for years. When you choose to be a soft place to fall, you don't just deepen your connection, you create a space where love can grow. And the beautiful bonus? He'll be far more likely to offer you that same grace when the roles are reversed.

Connection Key Three: Reboot Your Respect

The third key for supercharging your connection is to Reboot Your Respect—in other words, build up (or rebuild) the respect you feel for your man. You already know from chapter five that a man's greatest desire is to feel respected. But how do you increase your respect for him after it's dwindled or disappeared? That's where this key comes in.

The solution lies in your focus. What are you focusing on? When you notice your respect for your man dropping, it's usually because you're focusing on all the ways he falls short—what he's not doing right, how he doesn't measure up. This critical energy often snowballs, further eroding your respect for him and driving an even bigger wedge between the two of you.

If you want to reboot your respect, make the decision to shift your focus to what you appreciate or admire about your man. What is he doing right? What can you appreciate about him? What about him can you feel grateful for?

Maybe right now it feels hard to find something to appreciate—especially if he's spending hours gaming, or isn't working as hard as you think he should. But even in those moments, there are still small sparks you can build on. Maybe he takes the trash out without being asked. Maybe he's funny and makes you laugh on a rough day. Maybe he's quick to say yes when you need help lifting something heavy, or he brings you a cup of coffee in the morning. You don't have to force yourself to admire things that don't feel true, but shifting your attention to what is good—even if it's small—can start to change the energy between you. Where your attention goes, energy flows. Or said another way, what you focus on expands.

Here's the practice to Reboot Your Respect: In the mornings, take a few minutes to write down three things you appreciate about your man. Over time, as you focus on what you appreciate or admire, you'll begin to feel your respect for him increase. Your energy toward him will change, and there's no doubt your man will feel this energetic shift and respond in more appreciative ways toward you. If you'd like to take this practice one step further, invite your man to participate in the following exercise: At night before you go to bed, both of you share three things that you're grateful for or appreciate about each other from the day. You'll notice how giving and receiving this appreciation feels really good and creates a strong positive bond between you.

My friend Mary tried this practice with her husband, Steve, and found it extremely helpful for rebooting her respect for him, which had a remarkable effect on their relationship.

Mary

My husband, Steve, and I have been together for almost twenty years. Although there have been a lot of good times, there have also been stretches of fighting and tension between us when the relationship felt just awful.

Not long ago, we hit one of those rough patches. So rough that Steve was planning to move out for a while "just to take a break." Our frustration with each other was at an all-time high, and neither of us could take the nearly daily arguing and yelling.

Thank God for a trip we had already booked to Cabo San Lucas, Mexico. The tickets were bought, our lodging reserved—so, even with all our home-life drama, we decided to go. We always did better on vacation. Maybe it was the change of scene or just being more relaxed. Whatever it was, Steve and I had always been good at having fun together.

On our second day in Cabo, I found out that Tom, a man I knew from my work, was vacationing with his wife, Cindy, in the same area as we were. Tom was always raving to me about how much he loved Cindy and how happy they were. I was excited to finally get to meet her and see them together.

The four of us decided to meet for a walk at sunset on our favorite beach. Cindy was as lovely as Tom had said she was, and within minutes of being with the couple, I could see that they had a deep ease and affection for one another.

As we walked along the wide strip of sand, the waves lapping gently against the shore and the breeze ruffling the palms above our heads, our conversation turned to relationships. I just had to ask, "You two seem so happy. You're just radiating light and love. Are you really as good together as you seem?"

Smiling broadly, Tom said, "We are. It's just phenomenal."

"We feel so blessed every day," Cindy added.

"Wow," Steve said—and I thought I detected something wistful in his tone—"what's your secret?"

In unison, the couple said, "Appreciation!"

"What do you mean, exactly?" I asked.

Tom and Cindy told us about their daily appreciation practice. Every morning when they wake up and every night before they go to sleep, they tell each other one thing they appreciate about each other. Plus, at any time during the day that one of them feels they need or want some appreciation, they say to the other partner, "I'd love some appreciation right now." Even if the request is in the middle of an argument, they have an agreement that they'll stop and give the other person appreciation.

Steve and I turned to each other, a meaningful look passing between us. We knew all too well that we hadn't been very good at appreciating each other lately, so we made a commitment right there and then—to Tom and Cindy and to each other—that we would do this practice for the next thirty days.

We started that night! As we lay in bed holding each other, the moonlight streaming in the open window, I said, "I'll go first. Something I appreciate about you is . . ." I paused. "Your willingness to give this appreciation process a try!" Steve gave me a squeeze, and we both laughed a little.

It felt so nice, I just kept going, "Something else I appreciate about you is how you love walking in nature with me. And . . ." I was on a roll, "I appreciate how fun you are to be with!"

Steve smiled as he said, "Thank you, honey, that feels so good to hear. My turn now. Something I appreciate about you . . . is your enthusiasm for doing this appreciation process!"

We laughed again, then Steve went on, "I also really appreciate how patient you were with me today when I couldn't remember the password to the hotel account. And I appreciate how radiant you looked at dinner."

I thanked Steve with a long good-night kiss, and we settled down to sleep, feeling relaxed and happy. For the rest of the vacation, we continued the appreciation practice, always giving three or four appreciations each. And after we returned home, we kept it up, not letting anything get in the way of our new special us-time.

Our appreciations were often simple: something that one of us did that day, like Steve cleaning the kitchen unasked or my doing research on our house project, or something about our good qualities, like how kind Steve is to my family, or how dedicated I am to doing things well. What's amazing is that we heard things that we appreciated about each other that we never knew before.

As we showered one another with appreciation twice a day, our affection and comfort with each other grew, and Steve's plans to move out were put on hold. It felt so wonderful to be focusing on what was good, what was going right, what we loved and valued about each other.

Once we finished the thirty days we'd committed to, we didn't want to stop. We've been doing the practice every day—morning and evening—for more than six months now. And it has turned our relationship around! There's such a deep sweetness between us now.

Of course, we still have our arguments; we still have our annoyances, but they're all against the backdrop of appreciation. Because we're consistently focusing on what we like about each other, it's upped our ability to see all the good between us—which is far greater than the few things that aren't the best.

In fact, of all the many things we've done for our relationship—therapy, reading books, and taking seminars—I believe that this practice has created the biggest shift in our marriage. It consistently brings us back to a positive place with each other, smoothing the way for our love to deepen and flow.

Notice how all three connection keys—Love the Unloved, Be a Soft Place to Fall, and Reboot Your Respect—shift your energy toward more love, the first one for yourself, and the second two for him. As you practice these three keys, you'll notice both of your hearts opening even more. You'll feel the love between you strengthening and the trust between you increasing, and your conversations will become deeper and more intimate. Ultimately, you'll create a beautiful connection that continues to get stronger year after year.

GIFT BOX

Want an easy way to boost your self-love? Go here to download the "Self-Love Activation Toolkit" (which includes a special recording of Connection Key 1, the Self-Love Meditation Practice).

After more than a decade of coaching women in their love lives, I've found that the most painful conflicts in relationships are often caused by communication breakdowns. Yet we go through high school, often college, and in my case, even go on to earn a master's degree, and never receive one quality class on how to communicate with the people we love. The result of not learning this crucial life skill is that far too few of us have effective strategies for communicating. To quote one of my favorite comedians, Steve Martin: "Some people have a way with words, and other people . . . uh, oh, not have way."

The final part of the book is dedicated to giving you elegant and highly effective methods for communicating with your man so that you build bridges instead of walls and you both get what you want in the relationship with greater ease. Let's find our way with words, shall we?

Part Four

Speaking the Language of His Heart

Chapter Ten

The Art of MANguistics

Cheers!" my friend Jason said, clinking his beer bottle against mine.

It was a warm summer evening in Sun River, Oregon. The sun had already dipped below the horizon, making the pine trees appear black against the deepening blue of the twilight sky. The seven other guys sitting around the table also began clinking their bottles as "Cheers!" ping-ponged around the deck.

It was our twenty-fifth annual "Boys' Trip." Every summer since our senior year in high school, the nine of us had been getting together to reconnect and build our friendship. The trips started out as weekends away with just the guys. Twenty-five years later, our gathering included our wives and families and numbered thirty-three people—seventeen of whom were kids below the age of eight!

In those early years, we'd go camping, and each night, after a day of hiking, kayaking, or other outdoor adventures, we'd sit around the campfire and talk about anything and everything. It was a place where we could be completely honest with each other about our most personal feelings and experiences. Our usual topics included sports, college adventures, and our dream careers, but our favorite subject was always women.

In fact, on our very first weekend together, as our eighteen-year-old selves settled into a circle around the firepit, someone kicked off the after-hot-dog-roast conversation with the burning question, "So, how many times have you guys had sex?" After a pause and some snickering, a raucous and detailed discussion followed.

A quarter of a century later, even though we'd included the entire gang on this trip, we arranged for the women to have a girls' night and for us to have a guys' night—both without the kiddos.

It was our night to bond. Bags of chips and bowls of salsa were placed strategically around the table, and a platter of slow-roasted pork ribs served as the centerpiece. After twenty-five years, it was funny how some things had evolved, while others hadn't changed. Following our initial toast, the very first question was "So, how frequently are you guys having sex?" Laughter erupted around the table, and some friendly banter ensued, but eventually we all began to weigh in.

I listened to the replies, which ran the gamut from once a month to multiple times a day(!), then said, "You know, I learned something this year that was a total game changer for our sex life." All eyes turned to me. "I found out that Irene is totally fine with quickies! With three kids and work, sometimes that's all we have the time and energy for. It's crazy that after all these years of marriage, we never, not once, talked about it. We just assumed the other wouldn't be up for it. Talk about a failure to communicate. She's not only up for it—she's totally into it! Quickies have skyrocketed the number of times we make love." I shook my head. "Man, I wish I'd known that sooner."

A ripple of amusement ran through the group. "And on that same note," I said, my voice rising, "how come none of you f*%kers ever told me about the magic of coconut oil!?"

Everyone burst out laughing again and from around the table, I heard "Cuz you never asked!" and "We thought you knew!"

After the hilarity died down, my cousin Ty, who lives and breathes personal development, posed the next question, "Hey, what else have you learned this year that's helped your relationship?"

There was a beat of stunned silence and then a few playful groans, but our group is committed to being real, so everyone quickly leaned in, ready to share. Brian kicked off the conversation. "You know what's been a game changer for me? Giving my girlfriend a heads-up about our plans!

"I didn't realize how stressed it made Melissa when I sprang last-minute plans on her. One time I really screwed up: I invited her to a party my family was hosting, but we were already on our way there when I got around to mentioning that it was a potluck."

"Whaaaat?!" "Ouch!" "No, you didn't!" the guys called out.

"Yuuup, I did," Brian continued. "In the moment, I didn't think it was a big deal. We could just stop and buy something at the store, right? But I learned it was a big deal to Melissa because everyone else had homemade dishes, and she didn't get the chance to show how much she cared about my family by taking the time to cook something. I felt terrible.

"So now, I do my best to give her advanced notice on the plan for that week. And the more notice I give her, the happier she is and the smoother the ride is for everybody." In response, there were a few "Been there!"s and an "I hear you, brother!" from the group.

Riley went next. "My breakthrough was more about my stress levels," he told us. "When Becka and I both started working from home, she began doing something that completely threw me off. When I'm working on a project, I get super focused. It feels like my mind is a train locked into the tracks and going 100 miles per hour. The problem was, my sweet wife used to love to pop into my office and fire off questions. For example, she'd open my door and lean in to ask, 'Hey babe, what time should we leave on Saturday for your cousin's party?' To answer her, it felt like I'd have to figuratively slam on the brakes of my thought-train and switch tracks. And then, after we were done and I refocused on my project, just as I'd get back up to speed, she'd open the door again and ask another question, like, 'What do you want for dinner tonight?' It would drive me nuts!"

There was a chorus of agreement. "For sure!" "I hate when that happens!" "I'm with ya!"

He continued, "I explained the situation to her, and we came up with a system. Now, if she sees me focused on work and she's got a question, she simply asks, 'Hey, Riley, is now a good time? I have a quick question.' If it is, I stop what I'm doing and answer her. But if it's not a good time, I let her know how much time I need—which I can do without losing momentum on my work. It's a win-win."

Once Riley was done, we continued around the circle, and one by one, my friends shared their breakthroughs in their relationships. As I listened, I was struck by how many of them involved communication—or rather the lack of it. All the stories being shared were based on mastering that one vital skill.

That's why, in this chapter, you're going to learn the Art of MANguistics—specifically, five communication techniques based on the inner workings of the masculine mind and heart. These powerful techniques will help you and your man steer clear of any lurking relationship land mines and pave the road of communication, making travel smooth and easy.

What's more, the value of these concepts has been confirmed by the thousands of men attending my live events over the years, who on hearing them have burst into enthusiastic applause because they know that this information will help you connect to and understand them so much better.

MANguistics Technique One: Goal-ify the Conversation

In every conversation, your man has a particular goal he's trying to achieve. What is that all-important goal? To answer that question, we first need to understand the deeper motivations of the masculine and feminine when communicating.

Years ago, a friend of mine, relationship expert Dr. Pat Allen, shared with me a beautiful concept: A man's deepest subconscious desire is to have his thoughts respected, and a woman's deepest subconscious desire is to have her feelings cherished.

While it's true that everyone wants to be both respected and cherished, as you've already learned, the masculine prioritizes respect. He craves knowing that you believe he is enough and that he's the provider you want him to be. The feminine, on the other hand, prioritizes having her feelings cherished. She wants to feel seen and heard and know that her experience has been understood.

When couples aren't aware of these deeper desires when communicating, they can both end up feeling unloved and unappreciated—going round and round in arguments without giving their partner what they really need.

A common example of this is when a woman tells a man about a problem she's having. His first response, based on his masculine instinct to provide, is to try to give her a solution. For thousands of years the better a man could solve problems, the more his value would rise in the tribe. As a result, his self-worth is tied to solving problems. But often when you bring up a problem, while there are times you're looking for a solution, there are probably just as many instances when you don't need him to fix it—you simply need to feel seen and understood.

This concept baffles most men because most men don't communicate this way. If a guy brings up a problem he's having to a friend, it's for one reason—he's looking for advice! The idea that you just want him to understand and empathize with how you feel is as foreign to him as a hippo attempting ballet.

To help us understand why cherishing feelings comes naturally to you, and yet is so alien to your man, let's unpack our biochemistries. Remember how the feminine gravitates toward activities like communicating, collaborating, and connecting (for example, having someone acknowledge your feelings)? As you know, it's because all these activities stimulate oxytocin—the feminine's primary feel-good brain chemical.

The more you share and have your experience acknowledged, the more hits of oxytocin you receive. For the feminine, the longer and deeper the conversation, the better. The last thing the feminine wants when she needs to vent is for her man to give her a solution, bringing the conversation to an abrupt end.

In contrast, the masculine is drawn to activities like achieving goals, solving problems, and being efficient, which, as you remember, all trigger dopamine. For the masculine, the goal of a conversation is getting to the point you're trying to make. The masculine feels productive in a conversation if he can help you solve the challenge you're facing. The masculine gets his hit of dopamine by getting to the point and/or solving the problem, and, if he can do it more efficiently (or faster), then he feels even better!

To summarize, the feminine wants to extend the conversation, seeking as much connection as possible, while the masculine is champing at the bit to solve a problem and get to the point faster. This is why it can feel so frustrating when your man jumps in and gives you advice when you haven't asked for help. Or why your man gets that glazed look in his eyes when a conversation goes on too long for him. If he can't identify what the point is, or what problem you want solved, he gets restless and starts scrambling around his "apartmentalized" brain trying to figure out what his role in the conversation is.

Watching these conflicting agendas inevitably clash can feel like witnessing a slow-motion car wreck. Luckily, there's an easy (and simple) way to help you both get what you want in this situation. All you have to do is "Goal-ify the Conversation."

Here's how it works. You already know that men want to feel productive, and that they get this feeling by achieving goals. To harness this natural masculine motivation, tell him your goal for the conversation. Without knowing your goal, your man is certain to think up his own goal. And most likely, it will *not* be to simply connect.

So, from now on, when you're feeling frustrated and want to vent, say something like, "Honey, can I share what happened today? I'm not looking for solutions; I just need to vent for ten or fifteen minutes. That would make me feel really loved and supported. Would you do that for me?"

Notice a couple of nuances. Every goal includes these important components: 1) a clear outcome, and 2) a timeline. Using this technique helps your man hit the mark by telling him exactly what you want him to do. In this case it's to simply listen and not give you advice. When you give him a timeline, you help him prepare himself to be present with you the entire time you're speaking.

Over time, you can develop shorthand phrases to alert your man that you need to vent. These days, my wife will simply say, "Honey, I need some vent-time. Got ten minutes?" And I know exactly what I can do to help her feel better.

There's one more piece to this strategy that ties it all together: When you're done sharing and your oxytocin is on the rise, acknowledge your man for how he's helped you. This is important because for the masculine, just sitting and listening equates to doing nothing—in other words being useless, not a comfortable feeling for him. To counter this dynamic, simply say something like, "Thank you, honey. You're really good at making me feel better," and then finish with a loving gesture, like a sweet kiss or warm hug.

This last piece of acknowledgment is the payoff for the masculine: to know he's achieved the goal, and that he's helped you in some way. That's when he gets a beautiful hit of his feel-good chemical, dopamine. You'll be amazed at how following this MANguistics technique will turn him into a cherishing and listening machine!

To illustrate the effectiveness of this technique, check out this story from Aria, my cousin Ty's wife.

Aria

Ty and I run an organic farm together. It's a lot of work—both the physical labor and the job of managing our team of volunteers—but the two of us love it.

One day not long ago, I asked a group of volunteers to transplant one patch of strawberry plants into a different field, but when I came back to check on their progress, I found that they'd put the plants in the wrong field! As you can imagine, I was frustrated at the miscommunication and tried to straighten it out, but the conversation didn't go well.

Fuming, I walked into the house and began cleaning furiously, one of my go-to ways to dissipate my anger. Ty walked in and, noticing my agitated sweeping, asked me what was wrong. Trying to hold it together, I kept working but said, "I just wish people were more competent. Why don't people have a clue? Why don't they get it? What is wrong with people?" With each question, I gave the floor a vicious sweep of the broom.

Ty asked, "What happened?"

"I gave the volunteer team a project," I told him, "but it was completely done wrong. When I tried to correct them, they all got really defensive. Then the head volunteer threw his hands up in the air and said, 'I'm done. This isn't for me. Put someone else on this project!'" I shook my head, feeling frustrated all over again.

Ty looked thoughtful for a moment, then said, "Well, think about it from his point of view. If you're unsure of yourself and you were approached in a way that was critical, you can see how it would have been intimidating—especially because he was unable to meet your expectations. Hey, I'd probably feel that way, too . . ."

As he spoke, I could feel my jaw and stomach clenching as my anger got even hotter. I glared at him with a look so intense, I was surprised he didn't burst into flames right there, but Ty just continued giving me his suggestions,—"Maybe if you'd transplanted one as an example"—oblivious to the fiery fate that awaited him if he didn't shut up, and fast. Usually in this situation, I would end the conversation by saying something hurtful and storming out, but I suddenly remembered what I'd learned about asking him for what I needed and creating a goal for him.

I took a deep breath and, as calmly as I could, interrupted him. "Ty, that's all good advice, but what I really need right now isn't solutions—I know what I should have done. Instead, would you please just be on my side and hear me out for five minutes?"

Ty's eyes widened in surprise, but without skipping a beat, he said, "Oh, okay. Sure." Then he just looked at me, waiting for me to continue. When I did, he listened, every now and then interjecting, "That must really suck" and "I can totally see why you'd be frustrated."

Even though I'd asked him to do it for me, it was still so good to be heard and understood. When I was finished venting, I felt relieved, reassured—and grateful. A warm wave of love for my husband crested in my heart. Leaning the broom against the wall, I walked over to him and gave him a big hug. "Thank you."

Ty grinned at me, "That was great! I'm so glad I could help."

I smiled back. "You definitely did."

As you can see, this technique is simple but powerful. The hardest part is remembering to use it, because you're usually caught up in your own painful feelings when you need it. Of course, if you do want advice or solutions from your man, simply use this same formula and make "providing a solution" his goal. He'll be more than happy to oblige.

MANguistics Technique Two: Pause the Inner-Interrupter

Ever been chatting with your partner and see him get frustrated or shut down, and you don't know why? The problem is often that in your enthusiasm, you're jumping in with comments and reactions before he's finished speaking. If that's the case, this MANguistics technique might be the solution you're looking for—because there's nothing that shuts a man down faster than interrupting him while he's trying to make a point.

Of course, he shouldn't interrupt you either—good communication requires that both partners listen and respond to one another with love and care. And for the masculine, interrupting is especially painful. To encourage your man to open up more, here's a two-step formula:

Step 1: Let him start talking.
Step 2: Let him finish talking.

Okay, okay, I know that might sound flippant, but I promise it's not. On the contrary, this formula (especially Step 2!) is incredibly powerful for satisfying a man's deepest communication desire, which you now know is having his thoughts respected. The feminine communicator will naturally overlap conversations with her girlfriends, which means jumping in and adding her personal perspectives to what's being said. This serves to validate the other person's experience, and most women see jumping in and adding to the conversation as contribution.

Men, on the other hand, don't interpret interruptions as contributions to the conversation. They view interruptions as competition. Men typically interrupt each other when they are vying for alpha status. When you listen to his entire point without jumping in, it demonstrates that you value his perspective—in other words, that you respect his thoughts.

Plus, remember our lesson on biochemistry? Achieving goals gives your man a biological payoff. Getting to the point, finishing his story, or fully expressing his view is "the goal" of any conversation. Whenever he accomplishes that goal, he gets a little hit of dopamine. But when you interrupt him, it stops him from achieving his goal, which often feels frustrating for him.

To help him feel your love and support, use MANguistics Technique #2, Pause the Inner-Interrupter: simply notice when you feel the urge to jump in and share, then ask yourself, *Has he reached the point?* If he hasn't, pause the desire to interrupt and wait until he's completed his thought before contributing your perspective.

There's one more subtle and important aspect to this practice: If he's quiet for a few moments, don't take it as an open invitation to start talking. He's most likely gathering his thoughts, visiting other apartments in his brain to make sure there isn't an important point he's missing before returning to the apartment he's discussing with you. If you wait and are just with him in his silence, he experiences this as a huge expression of respect and will love you for it! And in future conversations, you'll notice that he naturally opens up more and more to you.

MANguistics Technique Three: Stick to One Tab at a Time

Once you start talking, there's a common conversation dynamic that confuses 99 percent of men—and which most women have no idea exists! Here's an example of what that dynamic looks like:

Jessica walked into the kitchen where Malik was sitting at the table, drinking his morning coffee. "Hi, honey," she said. "Do you have a few minutes to talk about our vacation?"

Malik's brows shot up. "Our vacation? Where are we going?"

"Nowhere yet, that's what I wanted to talk to you about." Jessica pulled out a chair and sat down across from him. "So, I talked to Amanda about Santa Fe—that's where she and Eric went last winter. Oh!" She put her hand to her mouth. "I forgot to tell you that Eric asked me if you wanted to come over and watch the game with him tomorrow. Do you want to?"

Malik rubbed his chin, considering this option, as Jessica continued, "Amanda told me they just bought one of those new big-screen TVs with surround sound. I wonder where they put it. They have so much art on the walls; I can't imagine where it will fit. Can you?"

Before Malik could weigh in on where the big-screen TV would fit, Jessica began speaking again, her tone wistful, "I'd really like to have more art in the house—especially a couple of big landscapes." She sat up straighter in her chair. "Hey, maybe I should take some lessons and try creating some pieces for our walls myself. I took that watercolor class and really enjoyed it. I gave one of my paintings to your mother. Do you remember?"

For a few seconds, Malik looked up at the ceiling, searching his memory but couldn't recall any painting. When he turned his attention back to Jessica to ask for more details about it, he saw she was looking at him expectantly. "Well," she said, "what do you think?"

Malik put his coffee cup down and stared at her. "About what?"

"About going to Santa Fe," Jessica said in a slightly exasperated tone. "Weren't you listening?"

If this type of exchange with your man feels at all familiar, consider using MANguistics Technique Three—pronto! This mismatch in conversational style and pacing is a common problem, a result of the different operating systems of the masculine and feminine brains.

As you already know from chapter eight, the feminine brain is like an internet superhighway, with every topic connected to every other topic. All you need to do to start a new topic in the conversation is open a new tab on the screen of your mind. It's normal to have thirty "tabs" open at any given time. Because. Every. Single. Tab. Matters. But as you deftly switch back and forth between subjects, opening new tabs before closing the tab you were previously discussing, your man likely finds it challenging to keep up with you.

That's because he's not using tabs. The masculine brain works like that large apartment complex, remember? The one where each apartment represents one topic in his life, and he can only be in one apartment at a time. So, to switch topics, he must exit the first apartment, walk down the hallway to the new apartment (aka new topic), open the door, and orient himself to discuss this new topic.

Inevitably, you'll want to go back to discussing the original topic, at which point, he'll have to exit the new room, walk down the hallway, and find the original apartment to continue the conversation. This kind of topic-switching is mentally exhausting for masculine men. A common complaint he has during a conversation is that his woman isn't being focused, whereas she gets frustrated because her man is too slow and can't follow her line of thinking!

Neither style is better or worse; they're just different. So if you want to support your man in staying more engaged in the conversation, use

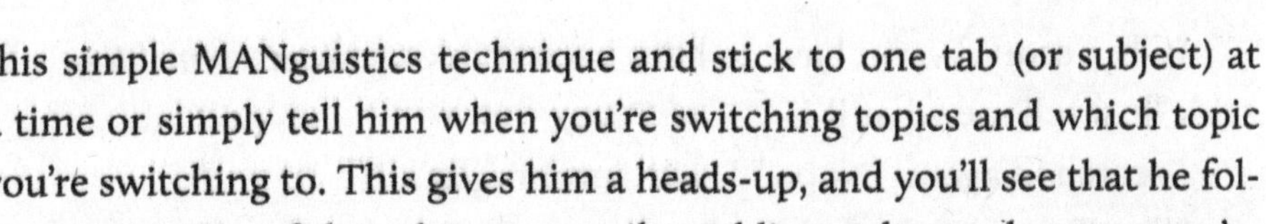

this simple MANguistics technique and stick to one tab (or subject) at a time or simply tell him when you're switching topics and which topic you're switching to. This gives him a heads-up, and you'll see that he follows your train of thought more easily and listens longer because you're helping him conserve energy.

The next technique is less about what to say, and more about what you can do to encourage your man to open up and share more with you in times of stress.

MANguistics Technique Four: Make Friends with His "Vacant Suite"

It's when the stress of life feels overwhelming that we need the most support from our partners. But that's often when the masculine and feminine collide because we naturally have different ways of managing that stress. When you understand your partner's approach to dealing with stress, you're better able to support each other.

Let's start with the way men deal with stress. The masculine mind has one very special suite in his apartment complex that men love. I call it "the Vacant Suite," because there's absolutely nothing in there—no topics, no tasks, no to-do lists, no agendas, no thoughts—*nada*. And that's just the way he likes it. This is the place your man goes when he simply needs to relax.

Destressing in the Vacant Suite is such a natural instinct for a man that he's often unaware he's in there until you ask him what he's thinking about. I learned this lesson myself many years ago. Not long after our wedding, Irene and I were driving to a family gathering on a Saturday. It had been a long, stressful week. About twenty minutes into our hour-long drive, after a few minutes of silence, Irene asked me, "Honey, what are you thinking about?"

I checked in, trying to identify any particular thoughts. Nothing came to mind, so I simply answered, "Hmm . . . nothing."

"Oh, c'mon . . . you have to have been thinking about *something*," she said. "Just tell me what it is."

I searched again. "Nope," I said, "nothing at all."

"Fine!" my wife huffed, folding her arms. "Don't tell me."

At that time in my life, I didn't know how to explain to her that I was in my Vacant Suite. It may feel challenging for a woman to accept that a man is not thinking about something, because she doesn't have the same Vacant Suite. Instead, the feminine internet-superhighway brain is always on—searching, scrolling, making new connections.

Like the actual World Wide Web, this is an awesome and powerful system—but there is a downside. When a woman feels stressed, she will often describe the experience as her mind "spinning"; searches popping up, tabs reopening, windows overlapping other windows, and she can't seem to shut it down. Sound familiar?

When you're stressed or overwhelmed in this way, one of the best strategies for unwinding is to hit the "share" button—sometimes over and over! The act of simply talking or sharing what's going on helps you calm your nerves and restores your peace of mind.

Can you see the paradox? When the feminine feels stressed, she wants to hit the share button and discuss all twenty-two tabs she has open. When the masculine is feeling stressed, he wants to retreat to his Vacant Suite and not talk about it. (Or if he's trying to solve an issue, he'll hole up in the one apartment associated with that topic until he's thought it through, and only then will he feel ready to share.)

Without a clear understanding of each other's stress-coping mechanisms, you and your man are bound to create more friction or feel rejected. One husband shared how he was stressed after a long day of work, and his wife encouraged him to talk about it. He told her he didn't feel like talking about it. As he walked into the bedroom to change, she followed him, saying, "I really think you'd feel better if you talked about it."

The truth is *she'd* feel better if he talked about it because communicating and connecting releases a woman's oxytocin. *He*, on the other hand, needs to visit his Vacant Suite first. "Making Friends with His Vacant

Suite" means not taking it personally if your man needs some alone time after a stressful day, and instead, supporting him by encouraging him to visit his Vacant Suite. This might be watching TV, chilling on the couch, going for a run, or working on a hobby—anything that doesn't involve him talking or interacting with anyone. Just twenty or thirty minutes of relaxing in his Vacant Suite can do wonders for reducing his stress levels and help him feel recharged and ready to give a much better version of himself to you. A small price to pay for such an enormous win-win.

MANguistics Technique Five: Give Him "Dopamine Time"

This technique helps your man shift his attitude to bring his best to your conversations. Like making friends with his Vacant Suite, it's less about what you say, and more about what you do. Ever have times when your man is grumpy, irritable, or in an overall bad mood, and neither of you can put your finger on what's causing it?

If you've given him the opportunity to visit his Vacant Suite and afterward offered to talk about what's on his mind, and his mood still hasn't improved, there's a good chance he just needs some good ol'-fashioned "dopamine time."

Getting together with his guy friends and doing something that requires focus, feels competitive, or feels productive gives your man a nice shot of dopamine, which will boost his masculine energy and help him feel better overall. And when his "d-levels" are high, something beautiful happens: he wants to return to you, ready to pour his newfound focus and energy on you—skyrocketing the overall quality of your communication and connection.

Savvy women have mastered this technique and notice when their man is in a crabby mood. They have a little alarm that goes off in their mind and they think, *Has he had much time with the fellas lately?* If not, they'll encourage their man to go get some dopamine time.

My sister-in-law Dora, who has been married to my brother John, a very masculine dude, for more than twenty-five years, recently shared a story with me about the power of dopamine time.

One day, early in their marriage, John came home from work in a terrible mood. His sales team had been struggling with plummeting sales results for the last two weeks, and it was getting to him. John stomped into the house, threw his bag down in the hallway, and trudged into the kitchen where Dora was making dinner.

Noticing his slumped shoulders and furrowed brow, she asked, "Tough day?"

"You think?!" John snapped. "These salespeople have no idea how to close a deal! We ended up getting one sale out of twenty presentations, and the worst part is—"

He was interrupted by their six-year-old twin daughters, Kiara and Kayla, who came running into the kitchen singing, "Who lives in a pineapple under the sea? SPONGEBOB SQUAREPANTS!" at the top of their lungs.

"Girls!" John shouted. "Will you please BE QUIET! I'm trying to talk to your mom!"

The twins immediately stopped singing and frowned as Kiara asked, "Why are you so grouchy, Daddy?"

Wrapping her arms around the two girls, Dora said, "Okay, let's go to the playroom, kids," and escorted them downstairs to give their dad some space.

Walking back upstairs, Dora wasn't happy about what had just happened, but she felt compassion for John. He'd been working so hard lately, without a lot to show for it. On top of that he'd been sacrificing the things he normally enjoyed doing for himself like golfing, working out, and playing poker with his buddies.

That's when Dora remembered that it was Wednesday—poker night! John had been too busy to play poker for over a month. Dora entered the kitchen and, seeing John sitting at the kitchen island, walked over and put her arm around his shoulders. "Hey, honey," she said, "are the guys getting together for poker tonight?"

"Yeah, I think so," he replied, his face etched with fatigue.

"Why not go?" Dora encouraged him. "I think it will be good for you."

"Yeah, you're probably right," he said, "but what about dinner and the twins' bedtime?"

"I'll take care of the girls tonight," she assured him. "You go bond with your buddies."

"Thanks, babe, I'll do that," he said.

When John got home from poker, it was as if a thousand-pound boulder had been lifted from his shoulders. Dora was brushing her teeth in their bathroom when John walked in with a big smile on his face. He came up behind her and wrapped his arms around her waist.

"Thank you! I definitely needed that," he said. "I'm so sorry for snapping at you and the girls earlier today. I've just been frustrated with work. Tonight was so good for me."

"I'm really glad," Dora replied, smiling back at him. She turned and gave him a kiss. "Now, go tuck the twins in. They're waiting for a goodnight kiss from their daddy."

"One hundred percent, I'm on it!" John said as he hurried out of the bedroom.

Some men enjoy playing poker, others prefer basketball, or golf, or soccer, or fishing, or working on classic cars—whatever the activity, dopamine time can feel like a magic elixir for a man, restoring his energy and reducing his stress.

Let's recap the five MANguistics Techniques:

1. Goal-ify the Conversation
2. Pause the Inner-Interrupter
3. Stick to One Tab at a Time

4. Make Friends with His "Vacant Suite"
5. Give Him "Dopamine Time"

I highly encourage you to test these techniques with all the men in your life: your father, brother, son, coworkers, and so on. Each technique is powerful on its own, but when you use all of them consistently, I know you'll be delighted at the result. Your man will be more open and more engaged—and don't be surprised when you hear him say something like, "Wow! Being with you is just so easy!"

There's one final piece about communication to discover before you've "officially" Cracked the Man Code: the best practices for resolving conflict with your man. Instead of arguing, giving him the silent treatment, or blowing up at him (for instance, after he informs you that the party you're en route to is a freakin' potluck!), the next chapter contains three proven conflict resolution practices that will help you dissolve even the biggest of disputes without drawing blood.

Chapter Eleven

Transforming Conflict into Closeness

Ashley and Curtis felt instant chemistry when they met online. They lived in different states, but that didn't prevent them from becoming extremely close—fast. They texted flirty and funny messages to each other throughout the day, then talked on the phone in the evening, often losing track of time, chatting until one o'clock in the morning. Within a few weeks, they shared a long romantic weekend together, which only intensified their feelings for each other.

Butterflies zinged in Ashley's stomach every time Curtis called. Curtis's heart swelled with excitement at finally meeting someone with this much potential. They had a ton in common: they shared the same faith, loved mountain biking, and both even had beagles! After three months and a couple more hot, whirlwind weekends together, Curtis decided to move to Ashley's town. To save money, they moved in together, deciding not to delay the inevitable, as they were already talking about marriage.

That's when the challenges began. Although Curtis and Ashley loved each other deeply and had a lot of fun together, they found themselves erupting into arguments on a regular basis. One night, Ashley returned home from the grocery store and placed a carton of milk on the counter.

"Ashley, are you kidding me? What is this?" Curtis asked, picking up the carton and letting out a frustrated sigh.

"It's the milk you asked for," Ashley replied.

"No, it's not," Curtis snapped. "I specifically asked for lactose-free milk. This is regular 2 percent milk. You know I can't drink this. It messes up my stomach." He set the carton down on the counter with a thud, his voice tight with irritation. "This is the third time you've brought home the wrong item in two weeks!"

"Oh, come on," Ashley told him, "Stop being such a baby. It's not that big a deal. I'll go back and get the right milk. You don't have to be such an assh*le about it."

Curtis took a deep, steadying breath. "Ashley, the fact that you don't think it's a big deal is the big deal to me. What if we have kids? How can I trust you to give our child the right kind of food if you can't get this little task right?"

"Whoa . . . hold on! Those are two completely different things," Ashley replied, her own temper flaring. "You're being totally unreasonable and a total jerk right now!"

"Well, I'd say you're the unreasonable one," Curtis shot back. "Why can't you just write these things down on a list like I've asked you to do a million times?"

"Oh jeez, not that again. You know what? I'm outta here. You can get your own damn milk!" Ashley stormed out of the house, slamming the door behind her. Tears streamed down Ashley's cheeks as she drove away. There were times she felt so close to Curtis, but fights like this caused her to doubt if they had what it took to make the relationship work.

Not long before she and Curtis met, Ashley had watched a few of my videos, so after several more painful arguments, Ashley reached out to me for help. She explained what had been going on, finishing with, "And if we don't learn better ways to handle our arguments, it won't matter how much chemistry or connection we feel—our relationship's over."

Fortunately, Ashley and Curtis's love for each other and their willingness to grow won out. Together, they learned the communication strategies you're about to learn in this chapter, which completely transformed their relationship—and the way they handle their disagreements. Ashley and Curtis are now happily married and have a baby on the way. While they still have their disagreements, they now have the strategies to defuse fights before they explode.

We all know great communication is vital for a healthy relationship. Unfortunately, when communication breaks down, very few couples have been given the tools to resolve the fallout. The hard truth is . . . conflict is gonna happen. Challenges, disagreements, frustrations, and arguments are inevitable in every relationship. But with the right practices, you can defuse any "conflict bombs" you face and steer clear of those painful "I-can't-stand-you-right-now" moments.

In this chapter you're going to learn three proven communication tools to use immediately with your significant other. And while these tools work phenomenally well with men, you can also use them to help defuse friction in any relationship in your life: your friends, parents, kids, siblings, coworkers, or unruly pet. (Okay, maybe not your pet . . .)

— Bomb Triggers 101 —

Have you ever started calmly discussing an issue with your partner, only to have emotions suddenly flare up, leaving the two of you at odds? You may have found yourself thinking, *How in the heck did we get here?!*

Chances are, one—or both—of you got triggered. The first vital step to resolving conflict is becoming aware of the behaviors that escalate disagreements into full-blown fights—or trigger the explosion of a conflict bomb, so to speak.

Here are five "Bomb Triggers," or actions that can provoke your partner and detonate a blast of emotion in an argument. Depending on how you were raised, these behaviors may seem normal or like "no big deal" to you; however, if you want to have a thriving relationship with your partner, mark these items down as "off limits" because they'll only escalate the conflict rather than resolve it.

Bomb Trigger #1: Name-Calling or Labeling

Name-calling is when you attack your partner's character with derogatory phrases like, "You're so lazy," "Don't be so stupid," or "You're acting like a total psycho right now." These words are like emotional daggers—they cut deep and leave lasting wounds.

Labeling is slightly different but just as damaging. Instead of targeting the person, you label their behavior in a way that's belittling or demeaning. For instance: "Leaving the dishes in the sink is so thoughtless," "Forgetting our anniversary was so incredibly selfish," or "Not texting me back yesterday was incredibly insensitive."

Even if these words are on the tip of your tongue in the heat of the moment, voicing them only intensifies the conflict and pushes your partner further away. Instead, you're about to learn how to transform those barbed comments into constructive, connection-building statements that actually get your needs met.

Bomb Trigger #2: Stacking the Past

An incredibly common argument tactic is to stack past offenses against your partner in an effort to build your case. Imagine this: you're frustrated that your partner didn't take out the trash—again. Instead of addressing that single incident, you unload a laundry list of grievances: "This is the fifth time you've forgotten something important! You didn't take out the trash last Thursday, you were late picking me up on Saturday, and you forgot our dinner plans two weeks ago! Why can't you ever get it together?"

While it may feel like you're proving your point, stacking the past only makes your partner feel attacked and defensive, escalating the conflict. Instead, keep the conversation focused on the present issue to resolve it faster and with less friction.

Bomb Trigger #3: Spouting "Always" and "Never"

Never use the term "always" and always avoid the term "never." Why? Because saying phrases like "You always do this" or "You never follow through" will trigger defensiveness in your partner. Someone being accused of "never" or "always" behavior will feel attacked and instinctively argue for any exception to your point.

Bomb Trigger #4: Flinging Sarcasm

Sarcasm is used to mock the other person and is degrading and hurtful. It relies not just on the words you use, but also on your tone of voice.

Examples of sarcasm:

"Right, you're *really* sorry for being late. I can tell."

"Oh, great, another brilliant plan. I'm sure this one will work just like the last five did."

"I know, you never make mistakes, because you're Mr. Perfect!"

The person being mocked will likely get defensive and retaliate against the sarcastic partner—derailing any progress the conversation was making.

Sarcasm is especially triggering for a person with masculine energy, since it's the antithesis of respect, and as I'm sure you remember, respect is paramount for the masculine. Avoiding sarcasm has another benefit for you: if a man feels respected, even while you're arguing, he's much more likely to respond with respect.

Bomb Trigger #5: Using the Communication Guillotine

A guillotine is a seriously intimidating device and a perfect metaphor for this bomb trigger. Its large, sharp blade drops quickly, slicing off the head of its victim, at which point the victim's thoughts, opinions, and perspective . . . well, don't matter anymore.

Using the communication guillotine during an argument means prematurely and abruptly cutting off the conversation by walking out of the room, hanging up on someone, or taking any other action in which you exit the conversation *without letting the other person know when you'll resume talking*. This act is like dropping an emotional blade on the interaction with your partner, cutting off the connection and sending the message that their feelings aren't important. It's another toxic communication strategy.

Please don't confuse using the communication guillotine with taking time to cool down and gather your thoughts so that you can circle back later when you're calm. That's a whole different—and productive—strategy for de-escalating conflict. But if you need a break to avoid saying things you'll regret, before you go, make sure to tell your partner when you'll rejoin the conversation. For example, you might say, "I'm getting really upset. I need thirty minutes to cool off and we'll talk about this again then."

It takes some discipline to refrain from cutting off the communication in the spirit of anger, but if you do, it'll go a long way to making the rift between you easier to bridge once you've both had a chance to simmer down.

The five Bomb Triggers are the primary ways people disrespect each other. Avoiding these behaviors keeps your conflicts from evolving into full-blown battles and helps raise the dialogue to a more effective and loving place. But it's not good enough just knowing what *not* to do. It's critical to have the right words and strategies to replace those behaviors. What follows are three proven communication strategies that will help you resolve conflicts more easily while maintaining a high level of respect for one another. To stick with our analogy, I've called them the Bomb "Defusers."

Bomb "Defuser" #1: Shovel While the Pile Is Small

If you've ever mucked out a horse stall, you know that shoveling manure is hard work—and that if you let the sh*t accumulate too long, it makes the job even harder. In the realm of relationships, the same wisdom applies: don't wait until a behavior or problem gets too big; instead, nip it in the bud.

This may sound counterintuitive because many of us were raised to not bring up an issue with our partner unless it's a big enough problem to discuss. In other words, don't rock the boat unless it really matters. I mean, who wants to risk being labeled "a nag" or "high-maintenance," or create unnecessary conflict, right?

Plus, if you're like most people who don't enjoy confrontation, you'll tend to let things go—even if they need to be addressed—hoping things change on their own. This type of "sweep-it-under-the-rug" mentality creates a situation where you push your feelings down over and over until the irritating event happens one too many times and then, KA-BOOM!—you explode, unloading our anger onto your partner, often throwing in their face all the times in the past they've done the same irritating thing.

This was certainly the case for Julie, whose husband Bill had a bad habit of leaving the kitchen cupboard doors and drawers open. Whenever Julie walked into the kitchen to cook a meal or grab a snack, she'd have to close at least one cupboard door and/or drawer to get to the part of the kitchen she needed.

Although Julie didn't like having to close the doors and drawers Bill left ajar, she didn't think it was a big enough deal to bring up. Julie had been taught to "pick her battles," and she didn't feel that Bill's absent-mindedness in the kitchen—which in the big picture was relatively minor and nonintentional—was a battle she needed to have.

Then one day, after years of closing Bill's open doors and drawers, Julie went into the kitchen to make herself some tea. She bent down to grab a box of tea bags from a lower drawer and when she stood back up, BANG! Julie whacked her head on the corner of an open cupboard door. To add insult to injury, when she tried to step to the side and move away from the cupboard door, CRASH! She banged her leg against a lower drawer that Bill had also left open.

That's when Julie lost it. Slamming the door and drawer shut, Julie stormed into the living room and let Bill have it.

"I am *so* pissed at you," Julie shouted at her startled husband. "You left the cupboard door open—for what must be the millionth time—and I bashed my head really hard on it. Plus, you always leave the kitchen drawers open, and I hurt myself on one of those just now, too. What is the matter with you? How can you be so inconsiderate?"

Bill, stammering apologies, felt terrible that Julie had been hurt. He also felt blindsided by her anger as he had no idea she had been closing the many doors and drawers he'd left open. She had never said one word before! Julie thought she had been doing the right thing by choosing not to share her feelings, but instead, it created a no-win situation with both partners feeling hurt and frustrated.

Letting things fester until you finally rage at your partner is a destructive communication pattern, because it erodes the trust in the relationship. The "perpetrator" ends up feeling unfairly attacked by their partner, having no idea how much their actions aggravated the other person until it's too late.

"Don't speak up unless it's a major problem" is seriously bad advice.

Instead, I encourage you to create an agreement with your partner that you're both willing to "Shovel While the Pile Is Small." That means make it okay to voice little frustrations while they're still "small" so that you can resolve them easily.

Here's a good guiding principle to determine when you should bring an issue up to your partner. If you're still feeling irritated (or stewing on an issue) twenty-four hours after it occurs, or if the irritating behavior repeats itself twice or more, then it qualifies as a "small pile to shovel" and it's important to bring it up as soon as possible so you can clear the air.

When you commit to shoveling while the piles are small, you'll notice that the conflicts you experience are less heated overall and get resolved a whole lot faster. To use this Bomb "Defuser," simply say, "Hey, honey, there's something I'd like to discuss so that I can shovel while the pile is small. This isn't a big deal; are you open to chatting?"

Here's an example of how it works:

One evening, I came downstairs after a long day of work and found the kids sitting in their high chairs and booster seats around the table, eating their chicken nuggets. When they saw me, they started cheering, "Daddy's done with work! Yaaaaaaayyy!"

Smiling, I kissed Irene and pulled up a chair next to the kids. We all started eating together. That's when I remembered that I hadn't checked to see whether my team had posted on our social media channels for that day. So I pulled my phone out of my pocket and began scanning my business's social media pages.

After a few minutes, from across the table I heard Irene say, "Honey, can I ask you for a favor? I'm shoveling while the pile is small here. The kids are so hungry for your attention. You've been working since 8 AM. Would you be willing to be fully present for them and put your phone down?"

Ugh, my heart sank with embarrassment. I'm usually the advocate for being present, yet there I was at the dinner table on my phone, disconnected from the family!

"You bet, honey, thank you for saying something. I need to finish checking this before tomorrow morning, but I can do it later, after the kids go to bed," I replied, putting my phone in my pocket.

"Thank you, babe," Irene said.

Turning my full attention to everyone around the table, I asked, "All right, family, what are your highs and lows from today?"

In any "small pile moment," you have a choice: you can address the issue with your partner, or you can repress your angst within yourself. But know this: *the quality of your relationship is directly related to the number of uncomfortable conversations you're willing to have.* Suppressing or ignoring your frustration only creates distance between you and your partner.

Irene's willingness to shovel while the pile was small not only helped me have a better connection with my family that night but also stopped her from bottling up her emotion about something and then exploding about the same issue later on. Your partner will always prefer the shoveling of a small pile over a volcano-sized eruption of pent-up emotion.

Bomb "Defuser" #2: The Do-Over

Have you ever said something harsh to your partner and immediately wished you could rewind time or take it back? Or "acted out" and thought, *Gosh, I wish I could redo that moment?*

Well, why can't you?

Remember when you were a kid playing games on the playground? If you were playing four square, for example, and another ball bounced into your game, messing up someone's turn, that person would yell, "Do-Over!" And everyone agreed that you'd start that point over. No big deal; it was just a Do-Over.

Here's the cool thing. Since your relationship with your partner is completely your own creation, you can set up the rules for your "relationship game" any way you want. So, why not allow Do-Overs? None of us are always at our best. When emotions like fear, insecurity, overwhelm, and stress creep in, it's easy to act negatively toward our partner, especially if we're tired. It's at those times that we can call for a Do-Over.

The trick to Do-Overs is to be self-aware enough to notice when your response isn't what the best version of you would do or say. In that moment, pause and take a deep breath. This creates some space between you and your response. Once you've taken that breath, consider what a more loving response would be, and ask your partner for a Do-Over.

A client of mine named Jill shared a beautiful example of the "Do-Over" in action.

Jill

My husband, Cris, and I really enjoy cooking together. It's our connection time—our fun zone. We love the teamwork, the dance-like maneuvering around each other in the small space, the back-and-forth banter as we chop, sauté, and stir. And to top it off, we get to eat all the delicious food afterward!

Since I work from home and Cris is retired, most of the time we cook our midday meal together. One day, as I made my way from my office to the kitchen to make lunch, I was feeling especially pressured. I had just finished a work call and had another one scheduled in just thirty minutes. Cooking and eating lunch in such a short window of time was going to be challenging.

Cris, who was in the family room, heard me come into the kitchen and appeared in the doorway, smiled at me, and asked, "What do you want me to do?" I had planned to make fajitas, so I asked him to chop the vegetables while I prepared the meat. He grabbed the peppers, onions, tomatoes, and mushrooms, and, standing at the cutting board, began slicing and dicing.

Opening the fridge to get the meat out, I realized I'd forgotten to take it out of the freezer! Oh no! Another delay when I was already racing against the clock. Frustrated, I whirled around, ready to grab the skillet to cook the meat, and stopped short. The cabinet with the pots and pans was directly below the spot on the counter where Cris was working at the cutting board, putting him smack dab in my way.

Sensing my presence behind him, Cris turned to me, an inquiring look on his face. Normally, I would have made a joke out of it, but today I was annoyed. "I need to get the skillet out," I said, my tone sharp. "Can you please move?"

Cris's eyebrows rose at my abruptness, but all he said was, "Okay, I'm just going to get out of your way," as he put his knife down and walked back into the family room.

"Great," I huffed under my breath as I bent down to retrieve the skillet. "Now I have to chop and cook . . ." But as I straightened up, I sighed, feeling my shoulders slump. Looking out the window, I thought, Cris isn't the problem. He just wants to spend this little pocket of time in our day together and I'm being a total grump. *I shook my head.* No wonder he left the room; I wouldn't want to be around me either.

I knew it was time for a Do-Over. Taking a deep breath, I walked into the family room, where I saw Cris watching the news on TV. I said, "Could I ask for a favor?"

With his eyes still on the screen, Cris said, "Sure."

Pointing toward the kitchen, I said, "That wasn't fun, and I don't feel very good about how I snapped at you. I would love it if we could try that again."

At my words, Cris turned to face me, with an expression I read as, "What would that look like?"

I smiled. "Just come back into the kitchen and I'll show you."

Returning my smile, Cris stood up, gave me a hug, then followed me back into the kitchen. As he took his place at the cutting board, I walked over to where I'd left the skillet and hip-bumped him playfully. Hip-bumping me back, he continued chopping, a big grin on his face.

We both laughed as we slipped back into our playful rhythm in the kitchen. We enjoyed a wonderful—and quick—lunch. And although the fajitas tasted great, it was our connection that I found the most satisfying.

The best part about the Do-Over is that it relieves the pressure of having to be perfect. At any moment, you have the ability to course-correct and the freedom to create a new—and better—outcome.

Bomb "Defuser" #3: The Sweaty 10-Minute Conversation

Remember how I said that the quality of your relationships depends on the number of uncomfortable conversations you're willing to have? Well, this last Bomb "Defuser" helps you know exactly what to say in those uncomfortable moments of conflict—the ones that make you sweat—so you can resolve the situation in a positive way.

The Sweaty 10-Minute Conversation tool was originally coined and created by my mentor, Dr. Gay Hendricks, and his wife, Dr. Kathlyn Hendricks. Over the years, I've applied this framework hundreds of times to heal rift moments in my own relationships and shared it with thousands of my coaching clients around the world. Believe me when I say that it's nothing short of transformational when it comes to resolving conflict. I've adapted the original framework just a bit to help "man-code" it—incorporating and emphasizing features that are important to the masculine mind and heart—making it even more effective to use in your relationship with your man.

Here are the five simple steps for having the "Sweaty-10," as I've come to call it. To clearly demonstrate what these five steps are and how to use them, imagine this scenario:

You and your man are living together. When he comes home from the gym, your guy has a habit of taking off his sweaty gym clothes and leaving them on the side of the bathtub. You don't enjoy moving his smelly, sweat-soaked clothes when you want to take a bath and have asked him to please put the clothes in the washing machine instead.

One particular day, you walk into the bathroom and see, yet again, his sweaty gym clothes hanging on the side of the tub. You feel irritated with this result and want to see it change.

NOTE: As we go through the Sweaty-10 steps, I encourage you to imagine applying this tool to a situation that's relevant to you.

Step One: State Your High-Level Intention

This first step works like magic to open your man up and help him be more receptive to what you're about to share. The last thing you want is for him to have his arms folded and be ready to defend himself at the outset of the conversation. So before launching into a litany of details about why you're frustrated, begin by stating your high-level intention for the conversation—the big-picture outcome you would most like to achieve by having this talk.

In our sweaty clothes scenario, let's imagine that your immediate intention is for him to put his workout clothes in the washer instead of on the side of the bathtub. Even though you're frustrated and want him to correct this specific action, ultimately you want a living situation that works for both of you. When you start the conversation by sharing a higher-level intention, it creates a more meaningful context for the entire interaction. It also gives your man the all-important goal he can achieve by having this conversation with you (a critical ingredient for his masculine operating system). Plus, a high-level intention encompasses what you and your man both want, putting you on the same team and avoiding a "you versus him" dynamic.

Here's an example of a great way to open your Sweaty 10-Minute Conversation:

"Hey, I'd like to have a Sweaty 10-Minute Conversation with you. My intention is to help us create a living situation that works well for both of us. Are you willing to chat?"

Here's a more universal high-level intention that you could use in any situation:

"Hey, I'd like to have a Sweaty 10-Minute Conversation with you. My intention is to create an even stronger connection and bond with you. Are you willing to chat?"

When he says yes to that question, you've helped him move to a more open and receptive state, you've given him the goal for the conversation, and you're both on the same team—which means, you're off to a productive start. Once you're both clear on the intention, move to Step 2.

Step Two: State What You See

Share exactly what you see and do your best to state only the facts. At all costs, avoid exaggerating, or using any of the bomb triggers (such as stacking the past, aka mentioning the previous times he's made the same mistake, or spouting "always" and "never"). Although these tactics are very tempting in the moment, as you learned earlier in the chapter, they generally backfire and make getting the outcome you want more difficult.

- If you exaggerate and say something like, "Your clothes are so stinky, I could smell them all the way downstairs in the kitchen!" he's likely to defend himself and debate the point: "I couldn't smell a thing until I came into the bathroom!"
- If you say, "You are always leaving your sweaty clothes on the tub," he'll point out the one time earlier in the week he did put his clothes in the washer.
- If you bring up the past and say something like, "I've picked up

your gross gym clothes for the past three weeks, and I'm sick of it!" he'll feel attacked and wonder why you didn't bring up the behavior the moment you wanted him to stop doing it.

Stating what you see (and sticking to the facts) is simpler and comes across a lot less charged. In this scenario it looks like this: "I came into the bathroom after breakfast and saw your wet gym clothes draped on the side of the tub."

Step Three: State How You Feel

After you share the facts, tell him how you feel. Here's a great tip: If your sentence is longer than three words, it's likely not a feeling statement but an opinion or judgment. Feeling statements are generally three words long and start like this: "I feel (emotion)."

For example, *I feel frustrated. I feel angry. I feel sad. I feel scared. I feel overwhelmed.* These are all effective feeling statements that get right to the main point you're making.

Here's a way to know when you're making an opinion or judgment statement: If your statement includes the word "like" or "that" after the words "I feel," then you've strayed into opinion or judgment-land.

For example, *I feel like you don't care about me. I feel like you're just being selfish. I feel like you're putting your needs ahead of mine. I feel that you're being a jerk.*

Can you see how opinion statements can come across as an attack? They'll certainly derail the conversation because, again, he'll likely get defensive and argue that what you just said is not correct. Here's the beauty about sharing a feeling statement. Feelings are not debatable. You feel the way you feel, and no one can tell you otherwise. End of story.

In this case, adding your feeling statement might sound like: "I came into the bathroom after breakfast and saw your dirty gym clothes draped on the side of the tub. *I feel frustrated.*"

Step Four: State What You Want

What change would you love to see? What outcome would make you happy, and what does it look like exactly? The clearer you are about what you want, the more likely he'll agree to what you're asking for.

Remember, men love missions—and the best missions are specific, measurable, and achievable. In our example above, you could say:

"What I would love is for you to put your sweaty gym clothes in the washer, and not on the bathtub, or to find some other solution so that I'm not the one picking them up."

Tell him specifically what achieving the goal and meeting your expectations looks like. Then give him a chance to respond, sharing his perspective and thoughts about the situation.

Step Five: Create an Agreement Together

Successful relationships are based on making and keeping clear agreements. In fact, the root cause of most arguments is an unclear, unspoken, or broken agreement.

If you want a different outcome in your relationship, then all you have to do is focus on one of these two actions: make a new agreement or recommit to an existing agreement.

Here's what this step looks like: after you've shared what you want, and your man has had a chance to share his thoughts about the situation—you're now going to identify the outcome you both desire, then turn that outcome into an agreement.

For example, you might start by saying:

"I came into the bathroom after breakfast and saw your dirty gym clothes draped on the side of the tub. I'm feeling frustrated. What I would love is for your sweaty gym clothes to end up in the washer and not on the bathtub, or to find some other solution so that I'm not the one picking them up. What agreement can we make that would work for both of us?"

Then let your man help co-create a solution. The goal is to agree on something that works for both of you. Once you've both come up with a plan, turn the plan into an agreement by saying something like, "That's a great idea. Can we make this our new agreement?" Or "Are you willing to recommit to our existing agreement?"

Creating a new agreement, or recommitting to an existing agreement, gives the two of you a fresh start and the confidence to know you can manage this situation based on clear shared expectations as you move forward.

Here's a quick summary of the five steps of the Sweaty 10-Minute Conversation:

1. State Your High-Level Intention
2. State What You See
3. State How You Feel
4. State What You Want
5. Create an Agreement

No matter whether you're dating or married or in a committed partnership, you can replace the sweaty clothes scenario with any one of a thousand other aggravating relationship moments. For example, you might be dating a guy who's not putting in as much effort as you are or doesn't give you enough notice when planning dates. Or perhaps you feel he's going too fast, and you want to slow the relationship down a bit. Or your guy committed to doing something and didn't follow through. The brilliance of the Sweaty-10 formula is that you can apply it to any situation where you want to see a change in the relationship or are feeling frustrated.

To give you an illustration of how this tool works in real time, here's the story of a "Sweaty-10" my wife brought to me right after we had our first child.

When Isabella was four months old, we installed a new baby gate at the top of the second-floor stairs to protect her from accidentally falling down the staircase. My home office just happened to be next to her bedroom on the second floor. Every day around 10:30 AM I would come down the stairs and head to the kitchen to refill my coffee. This also happened to be the same time Isabella was napping. If I didn't make a point to hold the gate, it slammed shut, sending a loud metallic "thwack" throughout the house—occasionally waking up the baby.

At this point in our new parenting roles, both Irene and I were very sleep-deprived, which made baby sleep-time a precious commodity. So the first time I let the gate slam and woke up Isabella, Irene gave me the death stare!

"Will you *pleeease* close the gate softly?" she said through clenched teeth as she walked upstairs to put Isabella back to sleep.

"Absolutely. I'm so sorry, babe," I answered, feeling horrible about wrecking nap time. Later that week, I finished a meeting with three minutes to spare before my next meeting started. Wanting to grab a quick cup of coffee before the meeting began, I sped downstairs and completely forgot about the gate.

I was already halfway down the stairs when, THWACK! The sound of the gate echoed throughout the house. I froze, and looked back upstairs, listening closely. I silently prayed to the nap gods that I hadn't woken the baby. After a few moments, all I could hear were the soothing waves of Isabella's sound machine. *Whew, I dodged that bullet*, I thought.

Irene was waiting in the kitchen with a frustrated look on her face. "Please, I'm begging you. Close. The. Gate. *Softly*."

"Yes, I'm so sorry . . . I raced downstairs and totally forgot about the gate," I said, quickly filling up my cup of coffee. "Okay, gotta go, I have a meeting starting right now." I dashed back upstairs, closing the gate quietly behind me this time.

The very next day, I finished a project and again had three minutes before the next meeting started. Hurrying downstairs for my refill, I forgot to hold the gate and THWACK! The gate closed hard. Horrified, I halted, straining my ears for any sound from Isabella. This time the nap gods weren't so forgiving. A soft cry came from Isabella's room, then grew louder and louder until it was full melt-down city. *Damn! How could I have forgotten the gate again?! We just talked about this!* I scolded myself.

Irene walked up the stairs—her energy cold as an arctic storm—and passed me without saying a word. She didn't have to. I could feel the bolts of rage shooting from her eyes and hear her unspoken tirade, *You've gotta be kidding me. I'm gonna kill you!*

Later that evening, when the baby was finally down for the night and Irene had had a chance to cool off, she used the Sweaty-10 brilliantly. We were sitting on the living room couch, about to watch a show we both liked, when Irene turned to me and said, "Honey, I'd like to have a Sweaty 10-Minute Conversation with you. And I want you to know that my intention is not to attack you but to help us create a different result so that you get what you need, and I get what I need. Are you up for that?"

"Of course," I said. The fact that she included my needs in her statement helped to lower my defensiveness. Not that I had much ground to defend, as I knew I was in the wrong. Even so, the feeling of my own energy opening, instead of bracing for the attack, was noticeable.

"Earlier today when you came down the stairs, the gate slammed and woke up Bella. I feel extreeeemely frustrated. It took me forty-five minutes to get her back to sleep."

"I'm sorry, honey. I feel really bad," I said, trying to own my side.

"We already had an agreement that you would close the gate quietly, so something isn't working here. What I would love is for you to keep that agreement and help Isabella stay asleep. What change could we make that would support you to do that?" she asked.

I noticed how much I appreciated her not "stacking the past." It would have been easy to call me out on the other two times I slammed the gate that week! She didn't have to stack the past to make her point. I had broken our agreement that day, and that was enough to ask for a change.

I thought about her last question, what would support me in keeping our agreement, and immediately had an idea.

"I got it!" I said, grabbing a pen and paper from the cupboard. I wrote

"SOFTLY" in big letters on the paper and walked upstairs and taped it to the gate. "This oughta do it," I said.

The next day as I raced out of my office for my morning coffee refill, the "SOFTLY" sign instantly grabbed my attention. I slowly closed the gate behind me and entered the kitchen without Irene even noticing I was there. I crept up behind her and softly hugged her and kissed her neck.

"Oh, who might this be?" she said in a playful tone, turning around.

"Your morning coffee ninja is in the house," I replied, giving her a sly wink. She laughed. I grabbed my coffee. And the baby enjoyed her nap.

I will be forever grateful to Gay and Kathlyn Hendricks for teaching me the Sweaty 10-Minute Conversation. Not only did it improve nap time for our little one, but over the years it's saved Irene and me from more than a few of our own "I-can't-stand-you" moments.

So, there you have it—three powerful Bomb "Defusers": Shovel While the Pile Is Small, Do-Overs, and the Sweaty 10-Minute Conversation. Each of these tools is designed to transform conflict into deeper connection, helping you navigate disagreements with grace and skill.

By recognizing and avoiding the five Bomb Triggers, you can prevent unnecessary blowups and keep communication clear and constructive. And by putting these three defusing strategies into action, you'll do more than just resolve conflicts—you'll build trust, intimacy, and a stronger bond with your man.

Over the course of these pages, you've been on a profound journey. You started by exploring the foundation of masculine and feminine polarity—the push and pull of attraction that ignites chemistry and keeps it alive. You learned how to stand in your feminine essence while inviting a man to show up fully in his masculine, creating that magnetic spark that draws the two of you closer.

From there, you moved into Ignition Attraction—the art of fueling his natural attraction for you in a way that feels effortless and magnetic. You discovered how to communicate your value, set healthy boundaries, and inspire him to pursue you in a way that feels both natural and exciting.

Next, you delved into Deepening Connection—the stage where chemistry evolves into genuine intimacy. You learned how to open your heart, create emotional safety, and nurture a bond that not only sustains love but also makes it thrive. You also explored how to invite your man to reveal his heart to you, fostering a deeper emotional connection.

Then, you finished with this section—Speaking the Language of His Heart—which showed you how to communicate in ways that inspire his love and devotion. You discovered how to avoid the Bomb Triggers that can derail even the best intentions, and how to use the Bomb "Defusers" to transform conflict into opportunities for growth and deeper intimacy.

Each of these sections has equipped you with powerful tools to create a relationship where you feel seen, valued, and cherished—and where your man feels inspired to love you deeply and consistently.

But at the heart of all these tools and strategies is one simple yet powerful truth: the quality of your relationships mirrors the quality of the love you give and receive. When you master your ability to love and be loved, you not only transform your relationships, you transform your life.

Before you journey forward and put all these tools into practice, there's one final message I want to share with you—a powerful reminder that ties everything together, helping you step more fully into the extraordinary relationship you're destined to create.

GIFT BOX

Want a pocket-sized cheat sheet with the Bomb Triggers and Bomb "Defusers" so you have them at a moment's notice? Download it here.

A Final Message

Someday, after mastering the winds, the waves, the tides, and gravity, we shall harness . . . the energies of love, and then, for a second time in the history of the world, man[kind] will have discovered fire.

—Pierre Teilhard de Chardin, nineteenth-century French philosopher

At the end of our lives, it won't be the "stuff" that we value: the cars, the clothes, the house, the money . . . none of it can be taken with us. Have you ever seen a U-Haul behind a hearse? Neither have I.

When it's finally our turn to leave this human experience, and we look back on our lives, I believe what will matter most will be the love in our hearts and the beautiful experiences we had with those we loved. Which is why I applaud you for reading this book! At its core, *Cracking the Man Code* is about deepening our capacity to love one another. So, congratulations on taking this personal step to lead with more love.

As you step forward from here, my hope for you is that you continue to practice these tools and principles, not just to build an amazing relationship with your man, but to expand your capacity to love and be loved in every area of your life. The ripple effect of love you create will extend far beyond your intimate relationship, touching everyone you meet.

As you integrate these principles into your life, you'll find that your man's heart will fill with profound appreciation for you. He'll feel deeply loved and respected, as if he were a king. And in true king form, he will treat you like the queen you are, loving and cherishing you like never before.

I'll leave you with one final client success story, written in her own words.

Kate

My husband, Paul, and I have been married for more than three decades. You'd be hard-pressed to find two people who are more opposite. I was raised in the suburbs of New York City, while Paul was raised in Montana, where, as he puts it, "there were more elk than people." I'm Jewish; he's Catholic. I'm highly verbal, while he dispenses information like a CIA operative—on a strictly need-to-know basis. Think Chatty Cathy marries the Marlboro Man.

These differences led to more and more conflict. As time passed, although I loved Paul, I often found I didn't like him very much, and that dislike ate away at the foundation of our marriage. For the first fifteen years, we muddled through; I survived mostly because I was surrounded by my longtime girlfriends, who supplied emotional support and soul-sustaining companionship on a daily basis.

But when we moved to a new town where I knew no one, it was just my husband and me. Together. All the time. With no one else to talk to. I found myself aggravated by his behavior, almost constantly, thinking, Can't he tell how I'm feeling? Why does he get so upset if I interrupt him? Why won't he hold up his half of the dinner conversation?

There was a lot of strained tolerance, punctuated by much eye-rolling, criticizing, and gritting of teeth on my part, and defensiveness and hurt on his. He felt attacked and disrespected, which closed him down even more. This negative feedback cycle was dragging us, day by painful day, closer to divorce.

I remember the incident that officially tipped me over the edge. We were in the car, on our way to Los Angeles, navigating stop-and-go

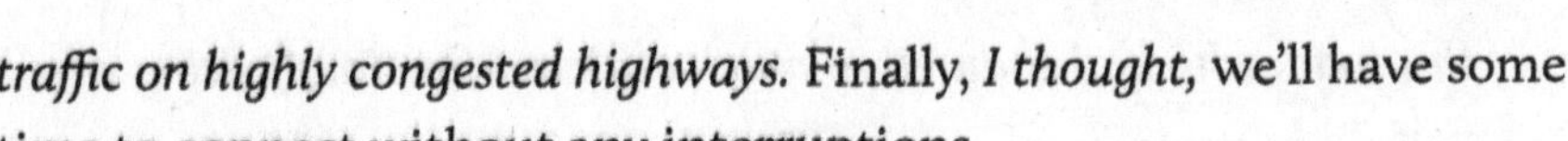

traffic on highly congested highways. Finally, *I thought,* we'll have some time to connect without any interruptions.

Turning to him, I said, "Hey, honey, how do you feel about your sister's new boyfriend?" It was a simple nonconfrontational question intended to give him a chance to tell me something he was feeling. A warm-up for more important topics I wanted to cover later on.

I sat, waiting for his response, admiring his handsome profile—the one that had driven me wild when we first met. The seconds stretched to a minute, then two. Crickets. Nada. No answer.

I spoke again. "Honey, did you hear me? I asked you what you felt about your sister's new boyfriend."

Keeping his eyes straight ahead, he said, "What?"

Trying to keep the irritation out of my voice, I said, "What do you mean, 'what?' Didn't you hear my question?"

Again, without looking at me, he said, "C'mon, not now. I'm driving and I need to keep my mind on the road and the traffic."

I closed my eyes, trying not to scream the words I was thinking inside: What is the matter with you? Can you really not do more than one thing at a time? *I was convinced there was something seriously wrong with his brain.* That's it, *I thought, holding back tears,* I can't stand this anymore. I'd rather be by myself.

But before I could get the legal machine of divorce in motion, by some marvelous stroke of luck, I went to a seminar on the Man-Code principles.

As I sat in the seminar room, my brain started going into hyperdrive, reviewing my husband's behavior and connecting all the dots. Our differences went beyond our personalities and upbringing—we were on opposite ends of the polarity spectrum. I suddenly understood the reason for all his confounding behaviors: He wasn't a defective female—he was a specimen of the masculine operating system!

Understanding that changed everything. I flashed back to moments in our relationship—including sitting in that car in traffic—and it all made perfect sense. I felt my heart swell with compassion and love for this man, who had endured so much criticism for simply being who he was.

I came home from the seminar that night to find him sitting on the couch, reading. Seeing him through this new lens of understanding, I felt shy—even a little awestruck—but mostly I felt guilty and terrible. I walked over and sat down beside him.

"Honey," I started, "I'm so sorry. I've been so horrible to you these last few years, and you don't deserve it." Then I burst into tears, sobbing too hard to continue. He took me into his arms and held me tightly, rubbing my back and murmuring soothing noises into my hair. It was the closest we'd been in months.

When I could talk again, I sat back and said, "You're an amazing man. I have so much respect for you," and then began explaining what I had learned about men. He listened carefully, his smile growing with each passing minute. "Can you ever forgive me?" I finished.

In answer, he leaned toward me and, taking my face in his hands, gave me a long, deep kiss—the kind of kiss that makes you melt inside. I kissed him back, wrapping my arms around him as we made up for lost time. The passion between us, which had been crushed by years of my disappointment and frustration with him, was back. It was like being newlyweds again—except better because we knew each other so well.

From that night forward, I stopped judging him and started appreciating—even admiring—him. His "bad behavior" explained, I started seeing the beauty and power of his talents and strengths. Of course, it hasn't been perfect all the time between us since then. We still have our personality incompatibilities that cause problems, but without the constant friction caused by my judgment of his masculine MO, our relationship has had room to breathe—and to blossom. Today, I not only love my husband, but I also genuinely like him. We laugh a lot and the ease between us is remarkable.

I've joined a new sisterhood, one that smiles on the "hunters" of the world and values their efforts to "protect and provide." This new appreciation of the masculine isn't limited to my husband. I see all the men in my life differently—including the ones I don't know but come across in daily life, like servers, grocery checkers, bank managers, salesclerks, even men I pass on the street. Not that all men are great—there are definitely some stinkers out there—but I finally understand that the vast majority of men are wonderful human beings whom I had simply been measuring with the wrong yardstick.

And while my new attitude toward men has certainly made interactions with me more enjoyable for them, it's been nothing short of miraculous for me. Because I approach men with positivity and openness, men are almost always kind and friendly to me in response, making my life feel safer, richer, and, ultimately, more fulfilling.

It's been an honor to write this book for you. My sincere hope is that the tools and concepts in these pages will help you "discover your fire" of love—igniting the passion, romance, joy, and connection in life that you so richly deserve.

If you find yourself wanting to take these learnings deeper, receive personalized coaching, or join a class designed to accelerate your progress, I invite you to visit www.love.bti.com/resources. You don't have to navigate this journey alone—you can have expert support, community, and guidance every step of the way.

Acknowledgments

I've come to believe that the secret sauce in life is gratitude. It's the fuel that powers our connections, the glue that holds us together, and the lens through which we see the true beauty in those around us. Writing this book has given me the perfect opportunity to pause and pour my heart out in appreciation for the people who have shaped this journey and filled my life with so much love and light.

To Irene, the love of my life and my greatest champion—the woman who's taught me what love truly looks like, not through words but through every act of kindness, patience, and unwavering support. You make me a better man every single day. Here's to a billion more magical moments together. I love you muchisimo.

To my kids, Isabella, Sephina, and Bryson—you are the heartbeat of my life. Thank you for pressing your little fingers under my office door, calling out "Play Time!" while Dad was in the writing zone. Your never-ending willingness to make up new dodge-sock games with Dad reminds me that life's best chapters are written in laughter, silliness, and all those precious, everyday moments.

To my mom and dad—thank you for giving me the greatest gift a child could ask for: a foundation of unconditional love. Even in the face of change, you led with grace, showing that love doesn't end when a marriage does. Long before the world had a name for it, you embodied what conscious co-parenting could look like—with mutual respect, heartfelt friendship, and a commitment to our family that never wavered. Because of your choices, we get to share holidays filled with joy, laughter, and unity. That is a rare and priceless legacy. I am forever grateful.

To my sister—a brilliant example of powerful feminine energy, living a radiant and joyful life. Thank you for being my earliest dating guru and for always leading with love.

To the Boyz Trip Group—you knew me back when I had the '90s hair, rocked the penny loafers with no socks, and thought I had it all figured out. Thanks for sticking by me then, and for still hanging out with me now.

To Gay Hendricks—your teachings have changed my life in more ways than I can count. Thank you for every powerful coaching moment, for every time you helped me see the possibility when I felt shaky, and for being a living example of what a conscious, love-filled life looks like.

To Carol Kline—for the countless early mornings, late nights, and *Outlander*-based Hidden Easter Egg jokes buried in the editing docs. You toiled over every word, every sentence, and every use of "deep" (like, a thousand times) to make this book shine. I'm forever grateful for your dedication and friendship.

To my Brave Thinking Family—you are soul partners in this mission to empower people to create and live a life they love. Your support and belief mean the world to me. Thank you for holding this vision with me and for bringing your light to everything you do.

To Ken and Helen Kleinberg—you believed in me when Jason and I were two clueless bachelors bumbling around the country interviewing married couples, and you've never stopped. Your support is a massive contribution to this work, and I'm so grateful for your unwavering belief in me.

To the beta readers—thank you for your unfiltered feedback and for helping me make this book the very best it can be. Your insights, honesty, and generosity have made all the difference.

To my beautiful online community—your comments, shares, and participation in spreading the message of love keep me going. You remind me every day that this work matters and that we're all in this together. Thank you for being an essential part of this journey.

To my clients—your courage and vulnerability in going after the love you desire inspire me every day. Watching you step up, lean in, and manifest the extraordinary reminds me why I love this work so deeply.

To Barbara Hinske, who wrote nineteen books in the time it took me to write this one—you are a dream achiever, and it's such an honor to be your coach. You inspire me each time we talk.

To the BenBella team—what powerful partners you are. Thank you for believing in this message and for helping to spread more love in the world.

And to you, the reader—thank you for choosing to pick up this book, for opening your heart to new ideas, and for being willing to grow. My hope is that every page you read brought you closer to the love you desire and deserve. May you go forth and love deeply, fiercely, and without reserve.

Cracking the Man Code Resources

If you're ready to take the principles from *Cracking the Man Code* even deeper, I've created some powerful resources to support you every step of the way. Whether you're looking to attract the right man, reignite the spark in your current relationship, or release old patterns that are holding you back from the love you desire, you'll find the right next step below.

Cracking the Man Code Online Course

Want to go beyond the book and master the communication strategies that deepen connection, overcome conflict, and ignite attraction? The Cracking the Man Code online course is your comprehensive guide to understanding the hearts and minds of men. You'll get step-by-step strategies to crack the code and create the kind of connection that lasts.

— Break Free Online Course —

If your heart has been bruised by the past—by heartbreak, betrayal, or disappointment—and you feel like something invisible is holding you back from fully receiving love, it's time to heal that wound at its root. The Break Free course is a transformational journey that gently guides you to release the old emotional pain and subconscious patterns that keep love at arm's length. As you clear these blocks, you'll reclaim your worth, restore your trust, and open your heart wide again—so you can finally let love all the way in.

— Manifest Your Man Coaching Program —

Ready to manifest the man of your dreams and live a life rich with love? Manifest Your Man is an in-depth coaching program that covers everything from attracting a high-quality man to creating a relationship in which you feel cherished, valued, and adored.

— DreamBuilder LIVE —

Imagine dedicating three days to focus solely on *you* and the dreams you have for your life. Whether it's finding the love of your life, deepening your current relationship, writing that book, or simply creating a life that feels vibrant, joyful, and fulfilling, DreamBuilder LIVE is where you bring those dreams to life. You'll join me and a community of like-minded, heart-centered people as we work through a proven system for turning your vision into your reality.

— Next Steps —

If you're ready to take your love life to the next level, and to learn more about these life-changing programs and resources, visit:

Notes

1 Nidhi Jaint et al., "Gender Based Alteration in Color Perception," *Indian Journal of Physiology and Pharmacology* 54, no. 4 (2010): 366–70, https://pubmed.ncbi.nlm.nih.gov/21675035/; Maris Fessenden, "Men and Women See Things Differently (No, Literally)," *Smithsonian Magazine*, March 31, 2015, www.smithsonianmag.com/smart-news/men-and-women-see-things-differently-literally-180954815/#:~:text=The%20results%20showed%20that%20women,that%20looked%20identical%20to%20men.

2 Ian J. Murray et al., "Sex-Related Differences in Peripheral Human Color Vision: A Color Matching Study," *Journal of Vision* 12, no. 1 (2012): 18, doi.org/10.1167/12.1.18; Shahenda Ayman, "Do Women See More Colors than Men?," *SCIplanet,* November 23, 2017, www.bibalex.org/SCIplanet/en/Article/Details.aspx?id=10304.

3 William O'Connor, "Why Did the Edge Walk Off the Edge? The Answer Might Surprise You," *Inside The Brain,* May 16, 2015, https://inside-the-brain.com/tag/peripheral-vision/; "Male vs. Female: The Brain Differences," A Brain Divided, Columbia University, accessed

June 12, 2025, www.columbia.edu/itc/anthropology/v1007/jakabovics/mf2.html.

4 Scott O. Murray et al., "Sex Differences in Visual Motion Processing," *Current Biology* 28, no. 17 (2018): 2794–99, doi.org/10.1016/j.cub.2018.06.014.

5 Adi Lausen and Annekathrin Schacht, "Gender Differences in the Recognition of Vocal Emotions," *Frontiers in Psychology* 9 (2018): 882, doi.org/10.3389/fpsyg.2018.00882; University of Montreal, "Women Outperform Men When Identifying Emotions," *ScienceDaily,* October 21, 2009, www.sciencedaily.com/releases/2009/10/091021125133.htm.

6 Linda M. Bartoshuk et al., "PTC/PROP Tasting: Anatomy, Psychophysics, and Sex Effects," *Physiology & Behavior* 58, no. 1 (1994): 1165–71, doi.org/10.1016/0031-9384(94)90361-1.

7 S. Rahrovan et al., "Male Versus Female Skin: What Dermatologists and Cosmeticians Should Know," *International Journal of Women's Dermatology* 4, no. 3 (2018): 122–30, doi.org/10.1016/j.ijwd.2018.03.002.

8 American Society of Plastic Surgeons, "Study Reveals Reason Women Are More Sensitive to Pain than Men," *ScienceDaily,* October 25, 2005, www.sciencedaily.com/releases/2005/10/051025073319.htm.

9 Denise Falcone et al., "Sensitive Skin and the Influence of Female Hormone Fluctuations: Results from a Cross-Sectional Digital Survey in the Dutch Population," *European Journal of Dermatology* 27, no. 1 (2017): 42–8, doi.org/10.1684/ejd.2016.2913.

10 Emily Henderson, "Dopamine May Help Explain the Gender Differences in Key Motivating Factors and Autism," *Medical and Life Sciences News,* June 24, 2021, www.news-medical.net/news/20210624/Dopamine-may-help-explain-the-gender-differences-in-key-motivating-factors-and-autism.aspx; Michelle Brandt, "Video Games Activate Reward Regions of Brain in Men More than Women," *Stanford Medicine News,* February 4, 2008, https://med.stanford.edu/news/all-news/2008/02/video-games-activate-reward-regions-of-brain-in-men-more-than-women-stanford-study-finds

.html; Carolyn Gramling, "Gender Gap: Male-Only Gene Affects Men's Dopamine Levels," *ScienceNews*, March 1, 2006, www.sciencenews.org/article/gender-gap-male-only-gene-affects-mens-dopamine-levels; Cam Adair, "How Dopamine Impacts Gaming," *Game Quitters*, accessed June 12, 2025, https://gamequitters.com/how-dopamine-impacts-gaming/; M. J. Koepp et al., "Evidence for Striatal Dopamine Release During a Video Game," *Nature* 393 (1998): 266–8, www.nature.com/articles/30498.; Yvonne H. C. Yau et al., "Are Internet Use and Video-Game-Playing Addictive Behaviors? Biological, Clinical and Public Health Implications for Youths and Adults," *Minerva Psichiatrica* 53, no. 3 (2012): 153–70, www.ncbi.nlm.nih.gov/pmc/articles/PMC3840433/; Judith E. Glaser, "Your Brain Is Hooked on Being Right," *Harvard Business Review*, February 28, 2013, https://hbr.org/2013/02/break-your-addiction-to-being#:~:text=When%20you%20argue%20and%20win,good%2C%20dominant%2C%20even%20invincible; Annemoon M. M. Van Erp and Klaus A. Miczek, "Aggressive Behavior, Increased Accumbal Dopamine, and Decreased Cortical Serotonin in Rats," *Journal of Neuroscience* 20, no. 24 (2000): 9320–5, doi.org/10.1523/JNEUROSCI.20-24-09320.2000; Nick Wolny, "Why You Love Setting Goals More than Pursuing Them, According to Science," *Fast Company*, August 4, 2021, www.fastcompany.com/90662001/why-you-love-setting-goals-more-than-pursuing-them-according-to-science; Ali Mohebi et al., "Dissociable Dopamine Dynamics for Learning and Motivation," *Nature* 570 (2019): 65–70, doi.org/10.1038/s41586-019-1235-y; Alice Park, "Why We Take Risks—It's the Dopamine," *TIME*, December 30, 2008, https://content.time.com/time/health/article/0,8599,1869106,00.html; David H. Zald et al., "Midbrain Dopamine Receptor Availability Is Inversely Associated with Novelty-Seeking Traits in Humans," *The Journal of Neuroscience* 28, no. 53 (2008): 14372–8, doi.org/10.1523/JNEUROSCI.2423-08.2008; Tim Newman, "What Happens in the Brain During a 'Eureka!' Moment?," *Medical News Today*, April 30, 2018, www.medicalnewstoday.com/articles

/321638; Martin Tik et al., "Ultra-High-Field fMRI Insights on Insight: Neural Correlates of the Aha!-Moment," *Human Brain Mapping* 39, no. 8 (2018): 3241–52, doi.org/10.1002/hbm.24073.

11 Alexandra Owens, "Tell Me All I Need to Know About Oxytocin," *Psycom*, September 23, 2021, www.psycom.net/oxytocin; Heon-Jin Lee et al., "Oxytocin: the Great Facilitator of Life," *Progress in Neurobiology* 88, no. 2 (2009): 127–51, doi.org/10.1016/j.pneurobio.2009.04.001; Shelly E. Taylor et al., "Relation of Oxytocin to Psychological Stress Responses and Hypothalamic-Pituitary-Adrenocortical Axis Activity in Older Women," *Psychosomatic Medicine* 68, no. 2 (2006): 238–45, doi.org/10.1097/01.psy.0000203242.95990.74; University of Haifa, "'Love Hormone' Oxytocin: Difference in Social Perception Between Men and Women," *ScienceDaily*, July 31, 2013, www.sciencedaily.com/releases/2013/07/130731093257.htm.

12 Steven W. Gangestad and Nicholas M. Grebe, "Hormonal Systems, Human Social Bonding, and Affiliation," *Hormones and Behavior* 91 (2017): 122–35, doi.org/10.1016/j.yhbeh.2016.08.005; Ailsa Harvey and Stephanie Pappas, "Oxytocin: Facts About the 'Cuddle Hormone,'" *LiveScience*, October 6, 2022, www.livescience.com/42198-what-is-oxytocin.html.

13 Meg Van Deusen, "The Power of Eye Contact: A Free and Easy Stress-Reducer," *Sight on Stress*, September 10, 2019, www.sightonstress.com/the-power-of-eye-contact-a-free-and-easy-stress-reducer/#_ednref1; Carol Sue Carter, "The Role of Oxytocin and Vasopressin in Attachment," *Psychodynamic Psychiatry* 45, no. 4 (2017): 499–517, doi.org/10.1521/pdps.2017.45.4.499; George Szasz, "The Science of Holding Hands," *BC Medical Journal*, September 26, 2023, https://bcmj.org/blog/science-holding-hands#:~:text=In%20practical%20terms%2C%20hand%2Dholding,to%20express%20feelings%20of%20closeness; Kerstin Uvnäs-Moberg et al., "Self-Soothing Behaviors with Particular Reference to Oxytocin Release

Induced by Non-Noxious Sensory Stimulation," *Frontiers in Psychology* 5, no. 1529 (2015), doi.org/10.3389/fpsyg.2014.01529.

14 Judith E. Glaser and Richard D. Glaser, "The Neurochemistry of Positive Conversations," *Harvard Business Review,* June 12, 2014, https://hbr.org/2014/06/the-neurochemistry-of-positive-conversations; Leslie J. Seltzer et al., "Instant Messages vs. Speech: Hormones and Why We Still Need to Hear Each Other," *Evolution of Human Behavior* 33, no. 1 (2012): 42–45, doi.org/10.1016/j.evolhumbehav.2011.05.004.

15 Kathleen C. Light, "More Frequent Partner Hugs and Higher Oxytocin Levels Are Linked to Lower Blood Pressure and Heart Rate in Premenopausal Women," *Biology Psychology* 69, no. 1 (2005): 5–21, doi.org/10.1016/j.biopsycho.2004.11.002; Kerstin Uvnäs-Moberg and Maria Petersson, "Oxytocin, a Mediator of Anti-Stress, Well-Being, Social Interaction, Growth and Healing," *Zeitschrift für Psychosomatische Medizin und Psychotherapie* 51, no. 1 (2005): 57–80, https://pubmed.ncbi.nlm.nih.gov/15834840/.

16 M. A. Hofman and D. F. Swaab, "The Sexually Dimorphic Nucleus of the Preoptic Area in the Human Brain: A Comparative Morphometric Study," *Journal of Anatomy* 164 (1989): 55–72, www.ncbi.nlm.nih.gov/pmc/articles/PMC1256598/.

17 Claire Sissons, "Typical Testosterone Levels in Males and Females," *Medical News Today,* January 6, 2023, www.medicalnewstoday.com/articles/323085?c=949257503991; David J. Handelsman et al., "Circulating Testosterone as the Hormonal Basis of Sex Differences in Athletic Performance," *Endocrine Reviews* 39, no. 5 (2018): 803–29, doi.org/10.1210/er.2018-00020.

About the Author

Mat Boggs is the bestselling author of *Project Everlasting* and the founder of Brave Thinking Institute's Love & Relationships division. As a leading voice in relationship coaching, Mat has been featured on *The Today Show*, CNN, *Headline News, The Style Network, Oprah & Friends*, ABC, and more. His engaging, research-backed insights into love and relationships have impacted millions worldwide.

For more than fifteen years, Mat has coached thousands of women, helping them create the love, connection, and commitment they desire. His signature blend of science-based strategies, heart-centered wisdom, and humor makes him one of the most trusted voices in relationship coaching today.